About the Marine Sanctuaries Conservation Series

The National Oceanic and Atmospheric Administration's National Ocean Service (NOS) administers the Office of National Marine Sanctuaries (ONMS). Its mission is to identify, designate, protect and manage the ecological, recreational, research, educational, historical, and aesthetic resources and qualities of nationally significant coastal and marine areas. The existing marine sanctuaries differ widely in their natural and historical resources and include nearshore and open ocean areas ranging in size from less than one to over 5,000 square miles. Protected habitats include rocky coasts, kelp forests, coral reefs, sea grass beds, estuarine habitats, hard and soft bottom habitats, segments of whale migration routes, and shipwrecks.

Because of considerable differences in settings, resources, and threats, each marine sanctuary has a tailored management plan. Conservation, education, research, monitoring and enforcement programs vary accordingly. The integration of these programs is fundamental to marine protected area management. The Marine Sanctuaries Conservation Series reflects and supports this integration by providing a forum for publication and discussion of the complex issues currently facing the sanctuary system. Topics of published reports vary substantially and may include descriptions of educational programs, discussions on resource management issues, and results of scientific research and monitoring projects. The series facilitates integration of natural sciences, socioeconomic and cultural sciences, education, and policy development to accomplish the diverse needs of NOAA's resource protection mandate.

Variation in Planning Unit-Size and Patterns of Fish Diversity: Implications for Design of Marine Protected Areas

Chiu-Yen Kuo and Peter J. Auster
Department of Marine Sciences and National Undersea Research Center
University of Connecticut, Groton

and

Jason Parent
Department of Natural Resources and the Environment
University of Connecticut, Storrs

U.S. Department of Commerce
Gary Locke, Secretary

National Ocean and Atmospheric Administration
Jane Lubchenco, Ph.D.
Under Secretary of Commerce for Oceans and Atmosphere

National Ocean Service
David M. Kennedy, Acting Assistant Administrator

Silver Spring, Maryland
July 2010

Office of National Marine Sanctuaries
Daniel J. Basta, Director

Disclaimer

Report content does not necessarily reflect the views and policies of the Office of National Marine Sanctuaries or the National Oceanic and Atmospheric Administration, nor does the mention of trade names or commercial products constitute endorsement or recommendation for use.

Report Availability

Electronic copies of this report may be downloaded from the Office of National Marine Sanctuaries web site at http://sanctuaries.noaa.gov.

Cover

Juvenile Acadian redfish (*Sebastes fasciatus*) at a boulder reef in Stellwagen Bank National Marine Sanctuary. Acadian redfish have relatively narrow habitat requirements. Spatial planning to conserve diversity must consider nesting multiple habitats within planning units in order to capture the greatest diversity in the smallest area. Image from University of Connecticut's ROV Kraken 2 courtesy of Peter Auster.

Suggested Citation

Kuo, C-Y., P.J. Auster, J. Parent. 2010. Variation in planning-unit size and patterns of fish diversity: implications for design of marine protected areas. Marine Sanctuaries Conservation Series ONMS-10-03. U.S. Department of Commerce, National Oceanic and Atmospheric Administration, Office of National Marine Sanctuaries, Silver Spring, MD. 52 pp.

Contact

Peter J. Auster, Department of Marine Sciences and Northeast Underwater Research Technology & Education Center, University of Connecticut at Avery Point, 1080 Shennecossett Rd., Groton, CT 06340 USA. Email: peter.auster@uconn.edu

Abstract

Marine protected areas (MPAs) have commonly been used to conserve or protect communities and habitats sensitive to disturbance, provide refuge for juveniles and spawning adults of exploited species, and serve as a hedge against management miscalculations or abnormal conditions. Species-richness hotspots are often used as an important focus for identifying conservation targets. We investigated how variation in planning-unit size (*i.e.* 10x10 km, 20x20 km, 40x40 km, and 80x80 km) affected spatial patterns of fish species richness and identification of diversity hotspots in the Gulf of Maine - Georges Bank region of the northwest Atlantic. Data from region-wide seasonal bottom trawl surveys from 1975-2004 were used to calculate total and mean richness estimates at each spatial scale. We found that planning-unit size and spatial variation in sampling effort had a profound influence on emergent spatial patterns of diversity. Spatial patterns of sample effort were uneven and contributed to variation in patterns based on total richness, especially at the smallest planning-unit size. A bootstrap approach was subsequently used to standardize effort and to estimate mean richness in each grid cell. Hotspots, defined as those planning units representing the top 10% of species richness, shifted from coastal areas to offshore sites with steep topography near Georges Bank at coarser planning-unit sizes, for both total richness and standardized effort approaches. Hotspots with similar species composition, based on cluster analysis, had discontinuous distributions at 10-km and 20-km scales. Regressions of analysis of similarity (ANOSIM) R values versus distance between hotspot pairs, at each planning-unit size, did not indicate any strong linear relationships. Furthermore, ANOSIM procedures at each planning-unit size showed that the 10-km scale had the highest species dissimilarity (based on Global R values) among individual hotspots. These results may be attributed to the patchy distribution of multiple species based on variation in habitat affinities and fewer habitat types occurring in small planning-units. It is difficult to conclude that a large MPA is better than several small MPAs; however, we suggest that increasing planning-unit size can reduce the effect of sample size on the selection of hotspots, increase confidence in the results of such analyses, and increase probability of encompassing representative species at regional scales.

Key Words

Spatial planning, GIS, biodiversity, hotspot, species richness, Gulf of Maine, Georges Bank, MPA

Table of Contents

List of Figures

List of Tables

Introduction

Marine protected areas (MPAs) are considered important management tools for conserving biological diversity in the sea in general and fishes in particular (Auster & Shackell 2000; Mora *et al.* 2006). Both empirical and theoretical modeling studies suggest that if properly designed, MPAs can aid in the conservation of species, populations, communities and habitats as well as the important biological and physical interactions that affect patterns of diversity and vice versa (Gell & Roberts 2003; Halpern & Warner 2002; Lindholm *et al.* 2001; Murawski *et al.* 2005). The potential benefits of protecting ecologically meaningful areas for marine conservation include: increasing the abundance, size, and fecundity of exploited species; spillover of propagules, juveniles and adults to serve as source populations to unprotected as well as other protected areas; maintaining the complexity and quality of habitats for sustaining populations and communities; conserving local examples of biological diversity; maintenance and restoration of community processes; and increasing resiliency from management miscalculations or abnormal conditions (Allison *et al.* 1998; Auster & Shackell 2000; Friedlander 2001; Roberts *et al.* 2003).

Much of what we understand about the performance of MPAs comes from studies of coral reef and kelp forest communities as well as other nearshore spatially complex habitats (Halpern 2003; Halpern & Warner 2002; 2003). In general, such studies demonstrate that protection increases populations of exploited species, habitat complexity, and biological diversity. While spatial management techniques have been used as tools across wide areas of continental shelf for marine conservation (*e.g.*, spawning closures for key species), the outcomes of such management approaches are not always clear-cut. Quantitative studies measuring the performance of MPAs indicate there are benefits for some but not all species and habitats (Collie *et al.* 2000; Lindholm *et al.* 2004; Link 2005; Murawski *et al.* 2005). For example, epifaunal communities on gravel substratum on Georges Bank demonstrate a positive response to closure attributed to the elimination of direct physical disturbance by fishing gear. In contrast, shallow sand communities in the same area (*i.e.* less than 80 m depth) have shown little demonstrable effect likely due to continued disturbance by tidal and storm currents and a resident fauna with life history patterns adapted to such disturbance regimes. MPA sites have been delineated using a variety of biological criteria (Auster & Shackell 2000; Botsford *et al.* 2003) including: (1) location of nursery areas and spawning sites for exploited species, (2) areas consistently utilized by highly migratory species including marine mammals, (3) areas containing habitats and communities important for key taxa or sensitive to disturbance such as seagrass meadows and coral reefs, and (4) areas of high biological diversity.

Conserving hotspots has become a primary goal for conservation as such sites include the greatest diversity, however measured, in the smallest area allowing other uses outside protected sites. However, diversity hotspots are defined in multiple ways including areas of high species richness, diversity (based on various indices of richness and evenness as well as higher level taxonomic relationships), and numbers of endemic or endangered species (Myers *et al.* 2000; Reid 1998). In any case species are not evenly distributed across space, so identifying hotspots requires data on species distribution. Many studies, primarily from terrestrial ecosystems, revealed that patterns of species diversity are strongly spatial scale dependent (Bohning-Gaese 1997; Connor & McCoy 1979; Lennon *et al.* 2001; Palmer & White 1994; Rahbek 2005; William 1986; Willis & Whittaker 2002; Zagmajster *et al.* 2008). This scale-dependent phenomenon is associated with one of the oldest paradigms in ecology, the species-area relationship (SAR), which demonstrates that species richness increases at a rate related to increases in the spatial scale of observation (Arrhenius 1921). For example, Lennon *et al.* (2001) demonstrated that diversity hotspots of birds in the United Kingdom move northwards when planning-unit size increased. This suggests that the choice of spatial scale for planning may be a critical factor for identifying the distribution of hotspots and meeting conservation objectives.

If scale-dependent changes indeed result in shifts in the actual location of hotspots, then identifying how and why such changes occur, and how conservation planning efforts might address such patterns, can aid the process of MPA site selection. Few studies have focused on the relationship between the spatial scale of observation and patterns of diversity in marine ecosystems. Herein we evaluated the effects of planning-unit size on emergent patterns of species-richness hotspots across the Gulf of Maine-Georges Bank Large Marine Ecosystem. We used data on the distribution of fishes as information for this taxon is the most geographically and temporally comprehensive due to their economic value and requirements for active and ongoing management. We also investigated both how spatial scale affects geographic patterns of species richness as well as the effect of sample size per planning unit on such patterns. An effort-standardization approach based on a bootstrap procedure was used to address variation in sample effort across the geographic region. In order to understand the equivalence of hotspots in terms of conservation value, we also investigated patterns of species similarity among hotspots across the gradient of planning-unit size.

Methods

The Gulf of Maine and Georges Bank (herein after the Northeast Large Marine Ecosystem or NELME) form a distinctive sub-region of the North American continental shelf (Sherman *et al.* 1996). Data on the distribution and abundance of fishes were obtained from shelf-wide research trawl surveys conducted by the National Marine Fisheries Services (NMFS) Northeast Fisheries Sciences Center from 1975 to 2004 (see Auster *et al.* 2006 for details of this data set). These multi-species surveys were designed to monitor trends in abundance and distribution of the demersal fish species inhabiting the region. Although these broad-scale trawl surveys cover continental shelf waters from Cape Hatteras to Nova Scotia, we focused this analysis on the NELME (Figure 1). Each station was sampled using a No. 36 Yankee (or similar) bottom trawl deployed for 30 minutes and towed at a speed of 6.5 km h^{-1}. Tows for each survey were conducted at 350-400 sampling stations using a stratified-random sampling design (NEFC 1988). Twenty-six strata were delineated based on temperature and depth (Azarovitz 1981; Grosslein 1979). Sample sites within strata were chosen at random for each survey based

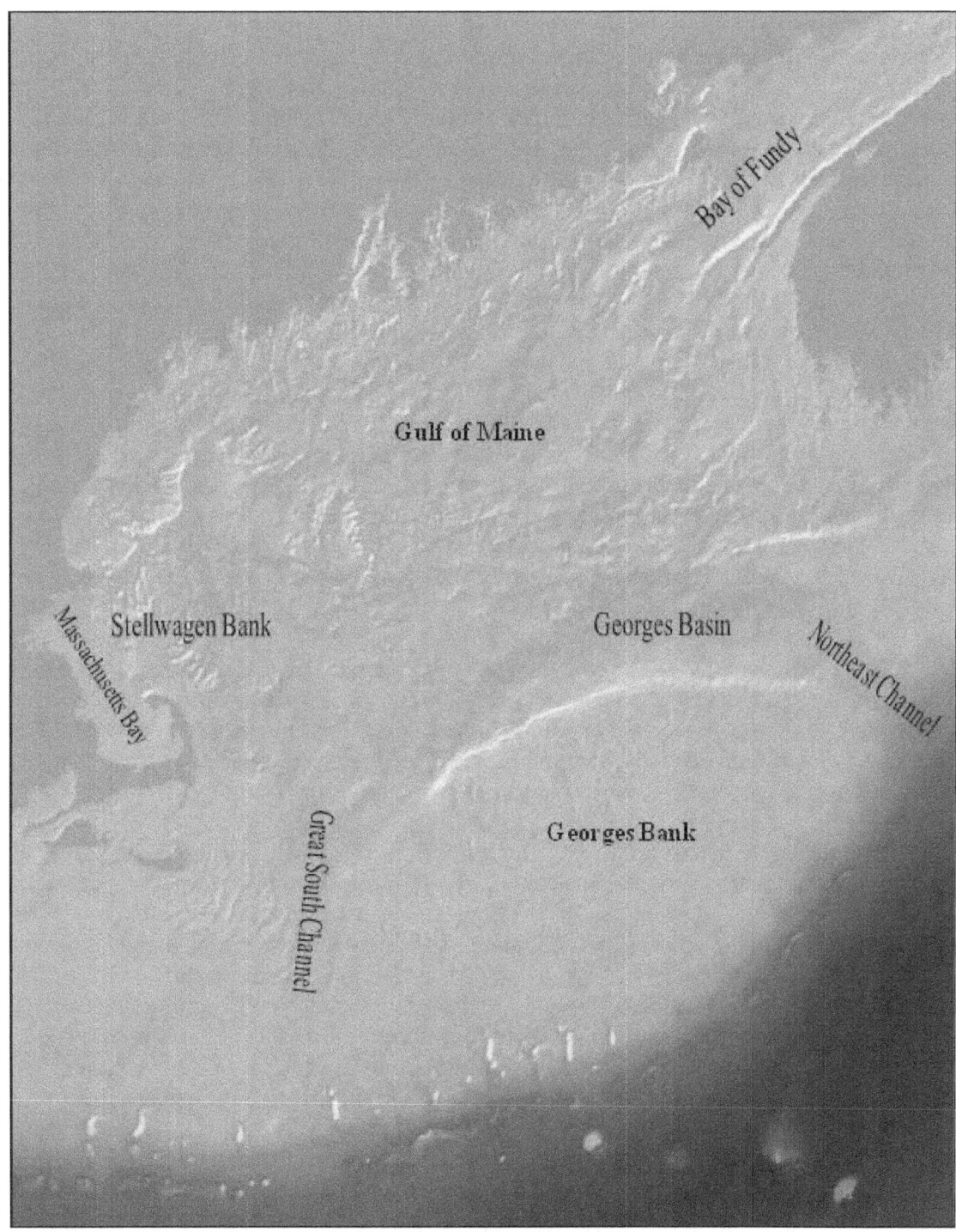

Figure 1. The Gulf of Maine and Georges Bank (NELME) region in the northwest Atlantic.

on one tow per 680 km^2 but with a minimum of five samples per stratum. Samples were collected in depths of 27 m to 350 m; however, greater depths were occasionally sampled in the deep canyons along the continental margin. Individuals in the catch were sorted to species, counted, weighed (to the nearest 0.1 kg), and measured (to the nearest cm). While sampling of northwest Atlantic fishes has routinely been done in all four seasons, the major focus has been in spring (March-May) and fall (September-November). Catch per unit effort (CPUE) was standardized for all tows. We aggregated data for both the spring and fall survey periods and across all years in order to produce a general perspective on patterns of species diversity in the NELME. A total of 7554 tows and 157 species was observed in trawl samples and included in the data set (Appendix 1 lists both scientific and common names).

In order to assess the role of planning-unit size on patterns of species richness, we partitioned sample data across seasons and years into grid cells at multiple spatial scales (*i.e.* 10x10 km, 20x20 km, 40x40 km, and 80x80km). The Create Vector Grid tool in the Hawths Tools extension in ArcGIS 9.1 (ESRI, Redlands, CA, USA) was used to produce uniform grids at each scale with trawl survey data linked to the geographic coordinates of each tow start location. Grid cells were nested, such that the smallest grid cell (*i.e.* planning-unit) was 25% of the size of the next largest unit, and so on. For example, a 20-km unit contained four 10-km units, thus survey data from four adjacent smaller cells were combined to estimate the species richness in the larger cell. For the NELME study area, there were 1353 planning-units at the 10- km scale, 366 planning-units at the 20-km scale, 106 planning-units at the 40-km scale, and 32 planning-units at the 80-km scale. Total species richness was then calculated for each planning- unit at each scale and plotted on a map. Patterns of spatial variation in species richness were identified by parsing the data into quintiles and plotting the results. Diversity hotspots were then identified as the planning-units in the top 10% of richness values, based on an *a priori* choice of threshold value (sensu Roberts *et al.* 2002), and serve as the primary focus of subsequent analyses. (Here the top quintile of richness values placed hotspots in a larger spatial context of high diversity sites and provides an example for use of alternative high diversity sites in the public process of negotiating locations of MPAs.)

The literature amply demonstrates the effects of sample size on estimates of species richness. In this study the random selection of sample sites within survey strata, as well as the practical limits on where trawl sampling can be conducted due to complex topography, resulted in an uneven distribution of samples across the region and between grid cells at all planning-unit sizes (Figure 2). This variable pattern of effort will be problematic for delineating diversity hotspots based on inclusion of planning-units as false positives and exclusion of units as false negatives. Further, the effects of variable effort will vary across the gradient of grid cell size since larger grid cells have larger sample sizes. To understand the effect of variation in sampling effort on the estimation of species richness we calculated sample size in each grid cell at each planning-unit size. The relationship between sample size and species richness within each planning-unit size was then calculated by using the curve estimation procedure in SPSS (SPSS Inc., Chicago, IL, USA) to determine the most appropriate regression model to fit the data. Further, in order to understand if the relationships between sample size per grid cell and species richness were significantly different at fine planning-unit sizes, models were compared using analysis of covariance (ANCOVA; Quinn & Keough 2003) to determine if there were significant differences among the slopes of the regressions. The null hypotheses that regression slopes are homogeneous, *i.e.* $\beta_{10km} = \beta_{20km} = \beta_{40km} = \beta_{80km}$, was tested by examining whether the interaction between grid size (categorical predictor) and

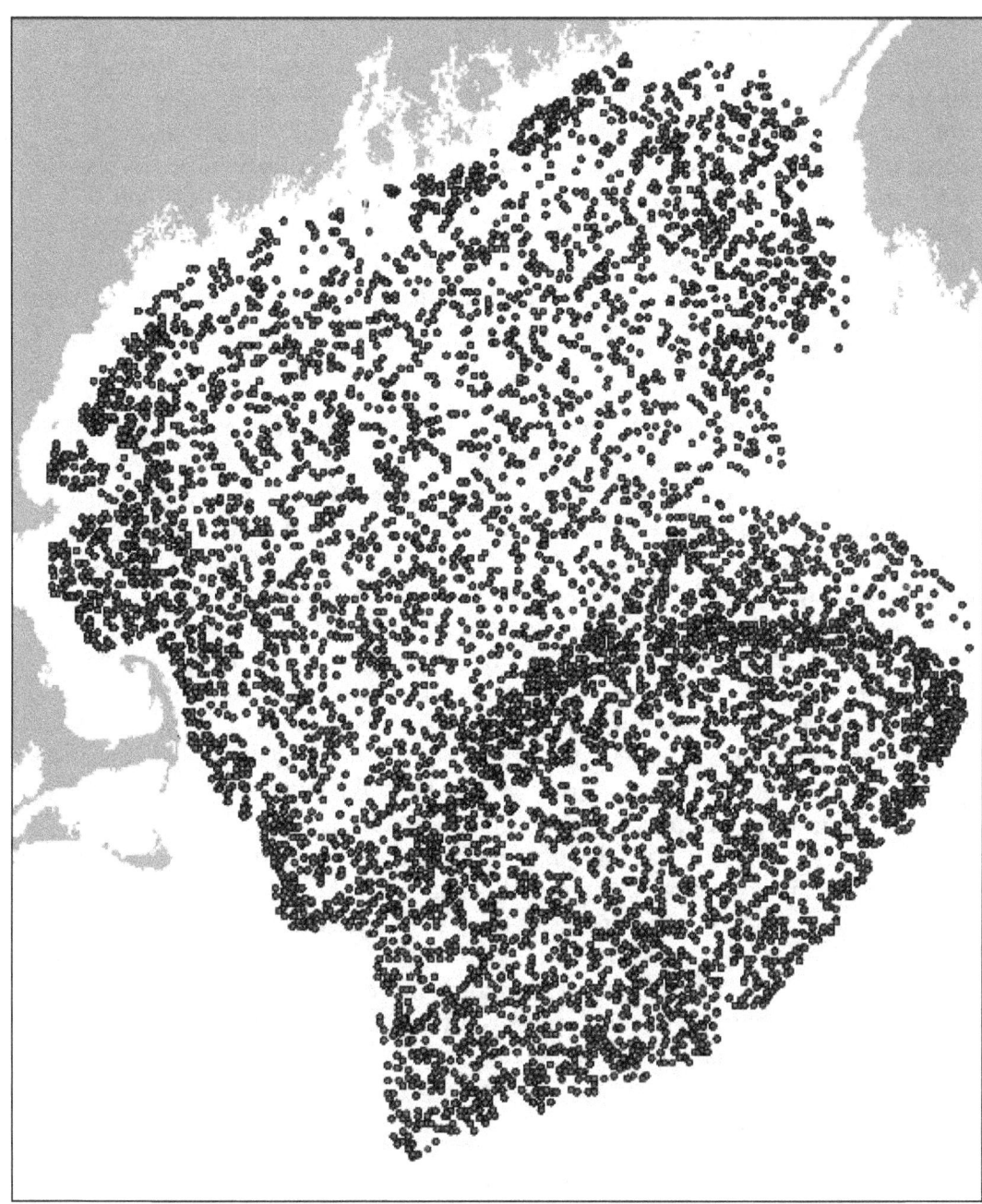

Figure 2. Location of trawl survey sample stations from 1975 to 2004.

sample size (continuous predictor) equals zero. When the results of the ANCOVA reject the null hypothesis, the Wilcox modification of the Johnson-Neyman procedure (Quinn & Keough 2003) was used to compare models in pair-wise groups to determine which regression models contributed to the difference.

To reduce the effect of spatial variation in this effort, we re-sampled the data using a bootstrap sub-sampling approach based on matching sample density across grid cells, at each planning-unit size. The appropriate sample size for each grid cell was determined by dividing the total area of each grid by 50 km^2 in order to accommodate grids along the coastal margin that contain less area then complete grid cells offshore. Data were then randomly re-sampled without replacement based on standard sample sizes. We chose sampling without replacement to maximize the probability of including all species, especially numerically rare species, from the samples in each cell. Grid cells were eliminated if the required sample size for re-sampling was larger than the actual sample size (180 grid cells for the 10-km scale, 54 for the 20-km scale, 22 for the 40-km scale, nine cells for the 80-km scale were eliminated). The effort-standardization procedure was repeated 1000 times in each grid cell and at each planning-unit size. Species richness in each cell was estimated by averaging the species richness calculated from each resample procedure. Species-richness maps were produced for each spatial scale and richness hotspots were identified as above.

Different hotspots may support the same number of species but the composition of species among hotspots may not be the same. To understand if species compositions were similar or different among the hotspots, we calculated Bray-Curtis similarity indices for all pair-wise comparisons of species composition (species and abundance based on numbers) in each planning unit from the bootstrap data set. We also visualized the similarities in species composition using hierarchical clustering and used the results to assign planning units to cluster groups for an Analysis of Similarities (ANOSIM; Clarke & Warwick 2001). The null hypothesis for ANOSIM is there are no differences in species composition between different hotspots. Alternatively, if two or more sample sites are different in species composition, then the dissimilarities between the groups should be greater than those within groups. The resultant global R value of this test is a measure of variation between samples compared to variation within samples with high R values indicating greater dissimilarity (Clarke 1993). Similarity percentage routines (SIMPER) were used to identify species that contributed most to the average dissimilarity between units. To understand how geographic distance between individual hotspots (i.e., individual planning-units) plays a role in similarity of species composition, we conducted an ANOSIM based on all pair-wise comparisons at each spatial scale. R values for each pairwise comparison were plotted against the geographic distance between planning units. If, in general, proximate planning-units were more similar then distal sites, then there should be a positive relationship between R and distance (i.e., less dissimilarity at short versus long distances). Abundance data were log(y+1) transformed and standardized between samples.

Results

Our results demonstrated that the locations of the species-richness hotspots varied with planning-unit size, both using observed patterns of richness and the effort-standardization method. Based on observed species richness, grid cells identified as hotspots were located primarily along the northern edge of Georges Bank and the coastal region of the western Gulf of Maine at fine scales (10 km and 20 km; Figures 3A and 4A). At larger planning-unit sizes, hotspots shifted from coastal areas to offshore sites with steep topography near Georges Bank (Figure 5A and 6A). There were only two hotspots identified at the largest planning-unit size and they were located along the northern edge of Georges Bank and the deep-water continental margin area along southern Georges Bank (Figure 6A).

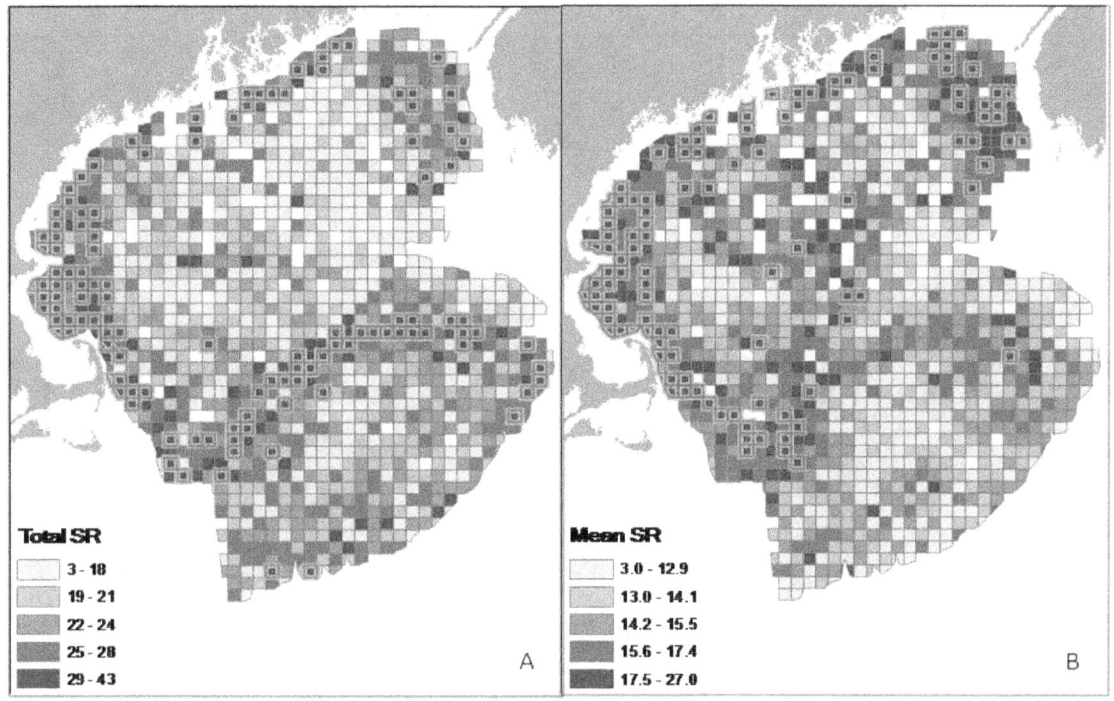

Figure 3. Spatial patterns of species richness at the 10-km scale: (A) total species richness (B) mean species richness based on the effort-standardization procedure. All planning-units are classified by quantile rank. The highlighted grid cells (blue) are those in the top 10 % of diversity values. Planning-units that did not have enough samples for the sub-sample procedure are blank.

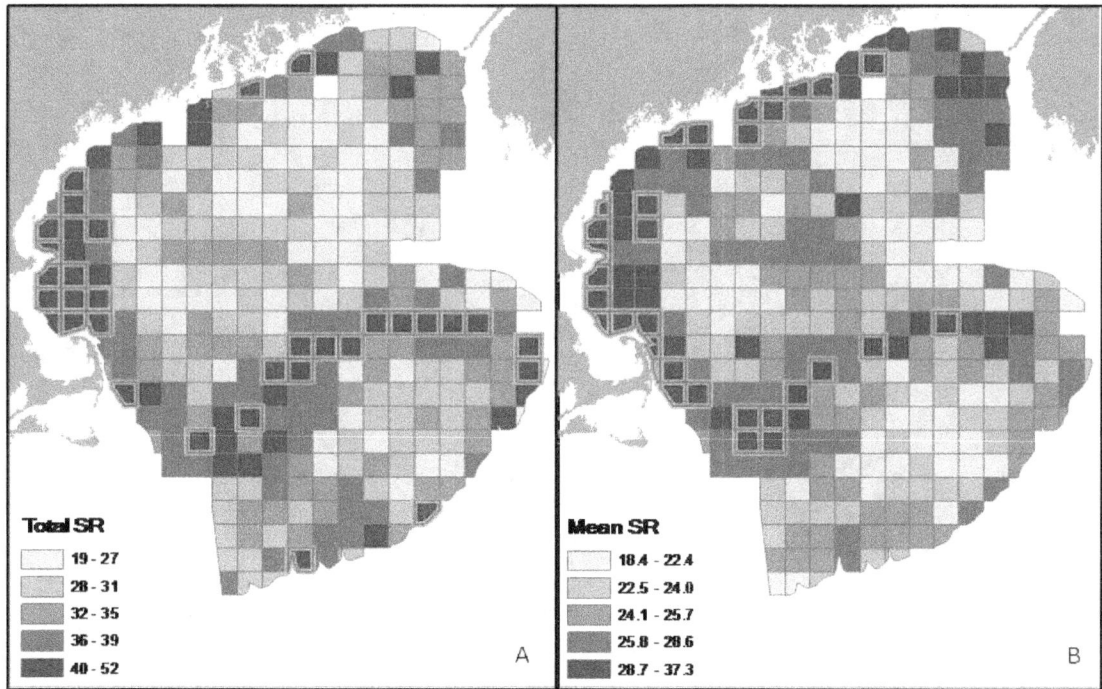

Figure 4. Spatial patterns of species richness at the 20-km scale: (A) total species richness (B) mean species richness based on the effort-standardization procedure. See Figure 3 for explanation of map details.

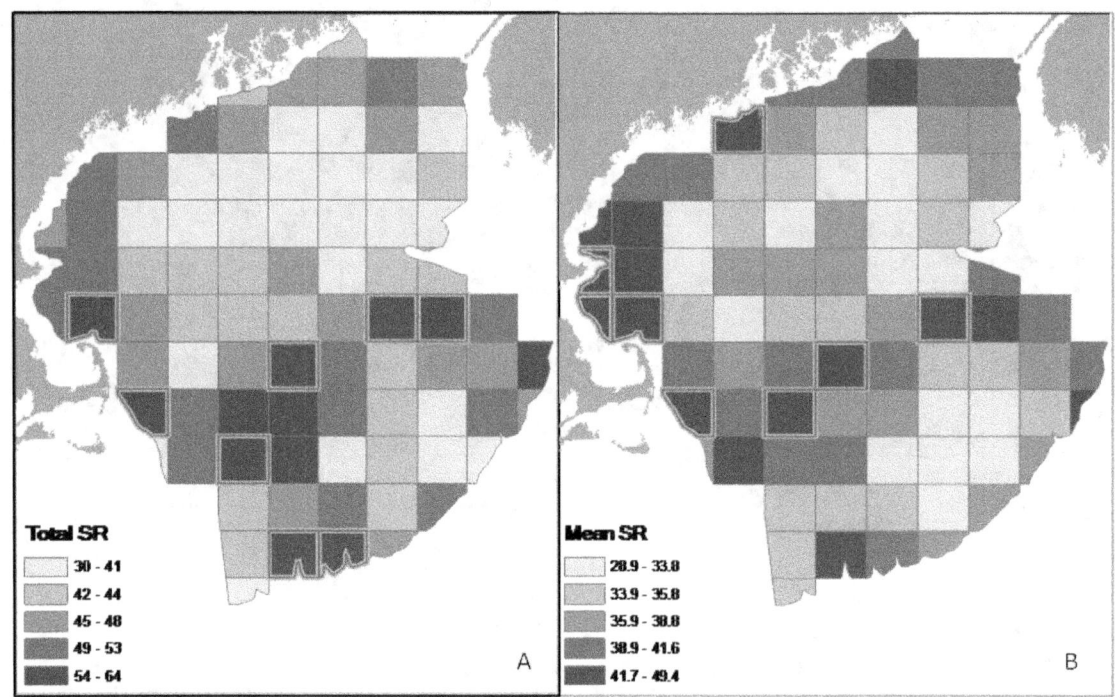

Figure 5. Spatial patterns of species richness at the 40-km scale: (A) total species richness (B) mean species richness based on the effort-standardization procedure. See Figure 3 for explanation of map details.

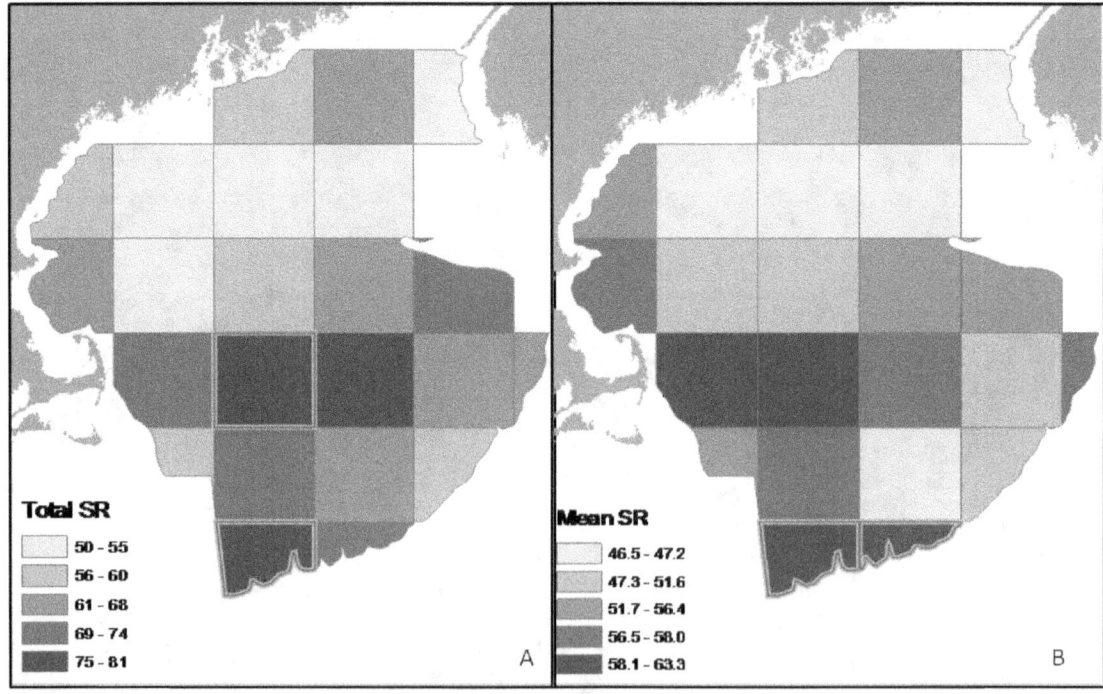

Figure 6. Spatial patterns of species richness at the 80-km scale: (A) total species richness (B) mean species richness based on the effort-standardization procedure. See Figure 3 for explanation of map details.

Not surprisingly, estimates of species richness in grid cells increased with sample size per cell (Figure 7). From the curve estimation procedure, power functions best described the relationship between richness and sample size between grid cells based on the highest r-square value and significance values (all significant at $p<0.05$, see detailed results in Appendices 2-5). Data were log_{10} transformed to perform further analysis. The results of ANCOVA indicated that grid size, sample size, and their interaction all had significant effects on the estimation of total species richness (Table 1). The significance value of the interaction between grid scale and sample size suggested that the regression slopes were significantly different. Comparison of the slopes of the power functions indicated that sample size has more of an effect on species richness when the sample size was small. The results of the Wilcox pair-wise comparisons indicated that the slope at the 10-km scale was significantly higher than that at all other scales (Table 2). A visual inspection of the resultant maps from the effort-standardization procedure show significant differences in the location of hotspots when compared to the results based on total species richness per cell (Figures 3-6). Approximately half of all hotspot locations shift based on the richness estimation method used for each cell regardless of scale (Table 3). From a geographic perspective at the 10-km scale, the hotspots along the northern edge of Georges Bank delineated using all observations disappear and new hotspots appear in the central basin of the Gulf of Maine and at more locations west of Nova Scotia based on the effort-standardization approach (Figure 3B). When the planning-unit size was increased to the 20-km scale, there was a pattern in reallocating hotspots from the north and south edges of Georges Bank to the coastal area (Figure 4B). At the 40-km scale, hotspots were found on northern and southern Georges Bank, and at two coastal sites along southern coastal Gulf of Maine based on observed richness. The southern Georges Bank sites disappeared and three additional hotspots were identified along the coastal region based on the effort-standardization procedure (Figure 5B). Species-richness hotspots were identified on the northwest and southwest edges of Georges Bank based on observed richness but shifted to the southern edge at the 80-km scale (Figure 6B). Overall, there was a shift in the location of hotspots from coastal areas to areas with steep topography as planning-unit size increased.

The number of hotspots decreased with increased planning-unit size but the total number of species appearing in the hotspots increased. 117 hotspots were selected by the sub-sample method at the 10-km scale, and 50 % of the fish species (79 out of 157 species) were included in the hotspots. 31 hotspots were selected at the 20-km scale, and 50 % of the fish species (79 out of 157 species) were included in the hotspots. Eight hotspots were selected at the 40-km scale, and 55 % of the fish species (86 out of 157 species) were included in the hotspots. Only two hotspots were selected at the 80-km scale, and 63 % of the fish species (99 out of 157 species) were included in the hotspots.

We assigned hotspots to either two or three groups based on the results of the cluster analyses, except for the 80-km scale that had only two hotspot planning units (Figures 8A-10A). ANOSIM Global R values represented the overall degree of similarity among cluster groups with a value of 1 indicating a maximum dissimilarity between samples.

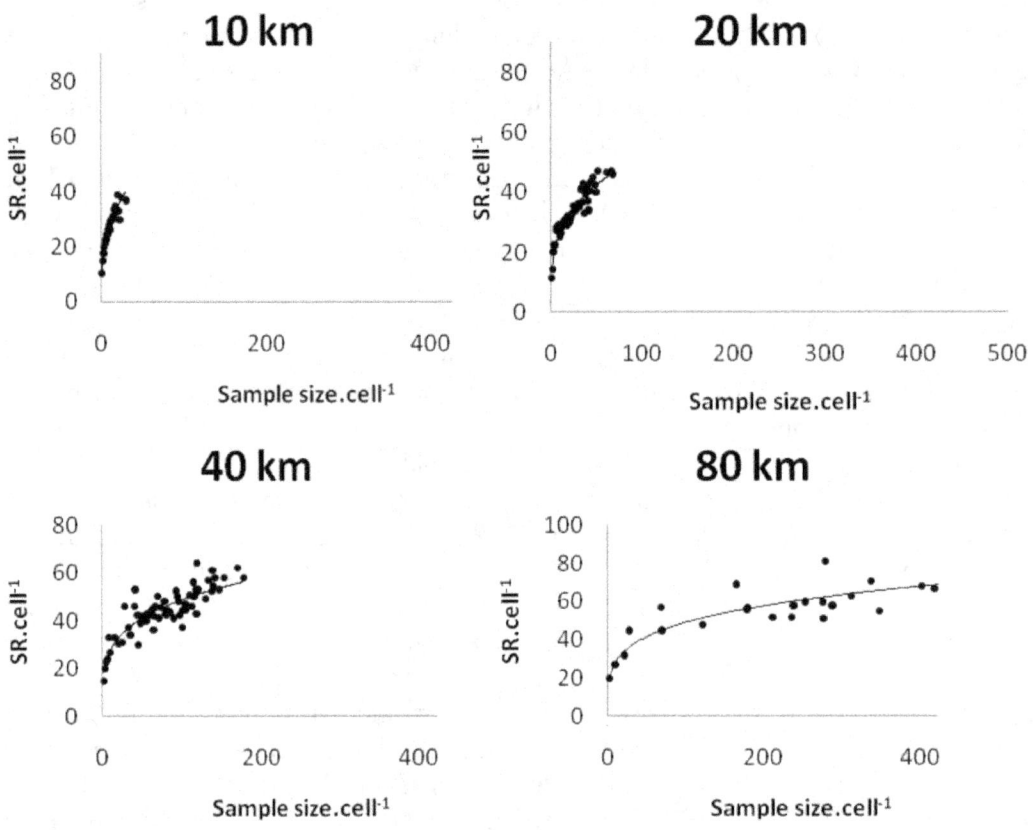

Figure 7. Relationship between sample size and species richness at multiple spatial scales. The best fits for the relationships between sample size and species richness at each spatial scale were: (A) $Y=11.6X^{0.354}$ ($R^2 = 0.927$, n=1262 , P<0.01) at 10-km scale (B) $Y=13.55X^{0.291}$ (R^2=0.9174, n=347, P<0.01) at 20-km scale (C) $Y=15.25X^{0.252}$ (R^2=0.8324, n=97, P<0.01)at 40-km scale (D) $Y=16.72X^{0.234}$ (R^2=0.8572, n=30, P<0.01) at 80-km scale. The results indicate that sample size in each grid cells has a positive effect on the patterns of species richness.

Comparisons of species composition among the cluster groups resulted in Global R values of 0.644 at the 10-km scale (P<0.001), 0.692 at 20 the km-scale (P<0.001), and 0.677 at the 40 km-scale (P=0.029). All comparisons suggested that species compositions were significantly different between any two of the hotspot groupings (based on a critical value of p=0.05). Figures 8B-10B illustrates the spatial distributions of the hotspot groups at each spatial scale. Hotspots with similar species composition, based on cluster analysis, had discontinuous distributions at 10-km and 20-km scales while the hotspots were separated along a north and south axis at 40-km scale. The results of the SIMPER analyses demonstrated that species that made the greatest contribution to the dissimilarity between hotspot groups for the 10-km, 20-km and 40-km scales varied in composition and percent contribution to dissimilarity (Tables 4-10). The contribution of individual species to the level of dissimilarity was relatively small (*i.e.* less than 5.5% maximum contribution).

Table 1. ANCOVA of planning-unit size, sample size in each cell (logSS), and their interaction on the estimation of species richness in each cell. In order to perform ANCOVA, logarithmic transformed valuables were used for species richness and sample size.

Source	Type III Sum of Squares	Df	Mean Square	F	Sig.
Corrected Model	43.550(a)	7	6.221	872.116	<0.001
Intercept	21.626	1	21.626	3031.506	<0.001
Planning-unit Size	.215	3	.072	10.064	<0.001
Logs	6.217	1	6.217	871.545	<0.001
Planning-unit * logSS	.630	3	.210	29.428	<0.001
Error	12.327	1728	.007		
Total	3321.909	1736			
Corrected Total	55.877	1735			

Table 2. Results of pair-wise comparisons based on Wilcox modification of the Johnson-Neyman procedure.

Pairwise comparisons	Significant range of covariate	Significance level
10 km VS. 20 km	logSS < 1.02	P<0.05
10 km VS. 40 km	logSS <1.46	P<0.05
10 km VS. 80 km	logSS <1.81	P<0.05
20 km VS. 40 km	-999.00	NS
20 km VS. 80 km	-999.00	NS
40 km VS. 80 km	-999.00	NS

Table 3. Summary of changes in the location of hotspots based on the observation of total species richness and the effort-standardization procedure. Total number of hotspots = number from all observations/number from effort-standardization procedure (hotspots were of equal number in both approaches); Number of stable hotspots = number of hotspots that did not shift locations between procedures; Percent constancy in location = number of stable hotspots/total hotspots.

Planning-Unit Size	Total hotspots	Number of stable hotspots	Percent constancy in location
10 km	117	55	0.47
20 km	31	13	0.41
40 km	8	4	0.5
80 km	2	1	0.5

Table 4. SIMPER results for comparison of hotspot group 2 versus hotspot group 1 at 10-km spatial scale. 27 species contributed to 80 % of dissimilarity (see Appendix 6 more details). The top 10 species are listed here.

Species	Av.Abund Group 2	Av.Abund Group 1	Av.Diss	Diss/SD	Contrib%	Cum.%
Helicolenus dactylopterus	0.06	1.02	1.74	3.29	5.42	5.42
Argentina silus	0.05	0.57	1.73	3.28	5.4	10.82
Myoxocephalus octodecemspinosus	10.96	0	1.72	3.3	5.35	16.18
Pseudopleuronectes americanus	2.56	0	1.45	1.84	4.51	20.69
Limanda ferruginea	3.48	0	1.17	1.34	3.64	24.32
Artediellus sp.	0.24	0.37	1.08	1.15	3.37	27.69
Brosme brosme	0.24	0.59	1.08	1.15	3.36	31.05
Enchelyopus cimbrius	1.69	0.11	1.07	1.15	3.32	34.37
Alosa sapidissima	0.3	0	1.02	1.1	3.18	37.56
Alosa aestivalis	2.11	0.07	1	1.06	3.11	40.67

Table 5. SIMPER results for comparison of hotspot group 2 versus hotspot group 3 at 10-km spatial scale. Thirty-six species contributed to 80 % dissimilarity (see Appendix 7 for details). The top 10 species are listed here.

Species	AV.Abund Group2	Av.Abund Group3	Av.Diss	Diss/SD	Contrib%	Cum.%
Enchelyopus cimbrius	1.69	0	1.25	1.62	3.89	3.89
Malacoraja senta	0.82	0.07	1.12	1.28	3.49	7.38
Leucoraja erinacea	0.96	6.66	1.02	1.13	3.15	10.53
Leucoraja ocellata	0.55	7.52	1.01	1.13	3.15	13.68
Alosa aestivalis	2.11	0.25	0.98	1.13	3.05	16.73
Alosa sapidissima	0.3	0.04	0.94	1.08	2.92	19.65
Triglops murrayi	0.62	2.29	0.93	1.05	2.9	22.55
Scomber scombrus	1.69	2.07	0.91	1.01	2.82	25.37
Hippoglossus hippoglossus	0.12	0.27	0.89	1.01	2.78	28.15
Ammodytes dubius	3.01	1.69	0.89	1.01	2.76	30.91

Table 6. SIMPER results for comparison of hotspot group 3 versus hotspot group 1 at the 10-km spatial scale. Twenty-nine species contributed to 80 % dissimilarity (see Appendix 8 for details). The highest top 10 species are listed here.

Species	Av.Abund Group3	Av.Abund Group1	Av.Diss	Diss/SD	Contrib%	Cum.%
Pseudopleuronectes americanus	23.76	0	1.94	8.55	4.99	4.99
Myoxocephalus octodecemspinosus	35.65	0	1.94	8.55	4.99	9.97
Helicolenus dactylopterus	0.04	1.02	1.82	3.56	4.69	14.66
Limanda ferruginea	8.47	0	1.81	3.58	4.66	19.32
Leucoraja erinacea	6.66	0	1.6	2.06	4.11	23.43
Brosme brosme	0.06	0.59	1.6	2.06	4.1	27.54
Aspidophoroides monopterygius	0.91	0	1.58	2.07	4.07	31.61
Leucoraja ocellata	7.52	0	1.57	2.07	4.03	35.64
Argentina silus	0.15	0.57	1.49	1.73	3.83	39.47
Triglops murrayi	2.29	0	1.14	1.16	2.92	42.39

Table 7. SIMPER results for comparison of hotspot group 2 versus hotspot group 1 at the 20 km spatial scale. Twenty-nine species contributed to 80 % dissimilarity (see Appendix 9 for details). The highest top 10 species are listed here.

Species	Av.Abund Group2	Av.Abund Group1	Av.Diss	Diss/SD	Contrib%	Cum.%
Lepophidium profundorum	0	0.31	1.16	21.69	5.13	5.13
Lumpenus lumpretaeformis	0	0.62	1.16	21.69	5.13	10.25
Lumpenus maculatus	0.11	3.07	0.93	1.94	4.11	14.37
Maurolicus weitzmani	0.12	0	0.81	1.49	3.58	17.95
Dipturus laevis	0.1	0	0.69	1.19	3.04	20.98
Tautogolabrus adspersus	0.14	0.8	0.59	0.97	2.62	23.6
Prionotus carolinus	0.26	0	0.58	0.97	2.57	26.18
Myoxocephalus aenaeus	0.13	0.03	0.58	0.97	2.56	28.74
Artediellus sp.	0.07	0.02	0.58	0.97	2.56	31.3
Pomatomus saltatrix	0.01	0.03	0.58	0.97	2.56	33.87

13

Table 8. SIMPER results for comparison of hotspot group 2 versus hotspot group 3 at the 20 km spatial scale. Thirty-five species contributed to 80 % dissimilarity (see Appendix 10 for details). The highest top 10 species are listed here.

Species	Av.Abund Group2	Av.Abund Group3	Av.Diss	Diss/SD	Contrib%	Cum.%
Cryptacanthodes maculatus	0	0.15	1	2.07	4.19	4.19
Lumpenus lumpretaeformis	0	0.38	0.97	1.91	4.09	8.28
Myoxocephalus aenaeus	0.13	0	0.72	1.19	3.03	11.31
Dipturus laevis	0.1	0.01	0.69	1.14	2.91	14.21
Lumpenus maculatus	0.11	1.77	0.66	1.09	2.79	17.01
Cyclopterus lumpus	0.04	0.08	0.65	1.07	2.75	19.75
Ammodytes dubius	33.97	1.74	0.65	1.04	2.73	22.48
Triglops murrayi	1.95	0.12	0.64	1.04	2.71	25.2
Brosme brosme	0.11	0.11	0.62	0.99	2.59	27.79
Prionotus carolinus	0.26	0.02	0.61	0.99	2.58	30.37

Table 9. SIMPER results for comparison of hotspot group 3 versus hotspot group 1 at 20 km spatial scale. Twenty-nine species contributed to 80 % dissimilarity (see Appendix 11 for details). The highest top 10 species are listed here.

Species	Av.Abund Group 3	Av.Abund Group 1	Av.Diss	Diss/SD	Contrib%	Cum.%
Lepophidium profundorum	0.01	0.31	1.05	2.85	5.16	5.16
Cyclopterus lumpus	0.08	0	0.79	1.45	3.85	9.01
Tautogolabrus adspersus	0.07	0.8	0.68	1.15	3.35	12.36
Maurolicus weitzmani	0.16	0	0.67	1.15	3.3	15.66
Ammodytes dubius	1.74	987.61	0.63	1.04	3.09	18.75
Triglops murrayi	0.12	0.06	0.63	1.04	3.06	21.81
Melanostigma atlanticum	0.06	0.01	0.59	0.98	2.87	24.69
Pomatomus saltatrix	0.01	0.03	0.59	0.98	2.87	27.56
Stenotomus chrysops	0.03	0.01	0.59	0.98	2.87	30.43
Ulvaria subbifurcata	0.6	0.41	0.59	0.98	2.87	33.31

Table 10. **SIMPER results for comparison of hotspot group 1 versus hotspot group 2 at the 40 km spatial scale. Thirty-five species contributed to 80 % dissimilarity (see Appendix 12 for details). The highest top 10 species are listed here.**

Species	Av.Abund Group1	Av.Abund Group2	Av.Diss	Diss/SD	Contrib%	Cum.%
Lumpenus maculatus	0	3.1	0.88	16.05	4.33	4.33
Helicolenus dactylopterus	0.24	0.01	0.68	1.68	3.35	7.68
Syngnathus fuscus	0.02	0	0.67	1.67	3.28	10.96
Stenotomus chrysops	0.01	0.02	0.66	1.66	3.24	14.2
Petromyzon marinus	0.02	0	0.66	1.66	3.21	17.41
Scomberesox saurus	0.05	0	0.56	1.25	2.75	20.16
Urophycis regia	0	0.1	0.55	1.24	2.7	22.86
Dipturus laevis	0.06	0.01	0.55	1.24	2.69	25.55
Merluccius albidus	0	0.03	0.55	1.24	2.68	28.22
Maurolicus weitzmani	0.05	0.13	0.46	0.97	2.23	30.45

Table 11. **Regression results for R value versus distance between each hotspot pair.**

Planning-Unit Size	N	R	Slope	P value
10 km	6785	0.114	0.001	<0.001
20 km	464	0.059	0.001	<0.001
40 km	27	0.002	8E-005	0.836

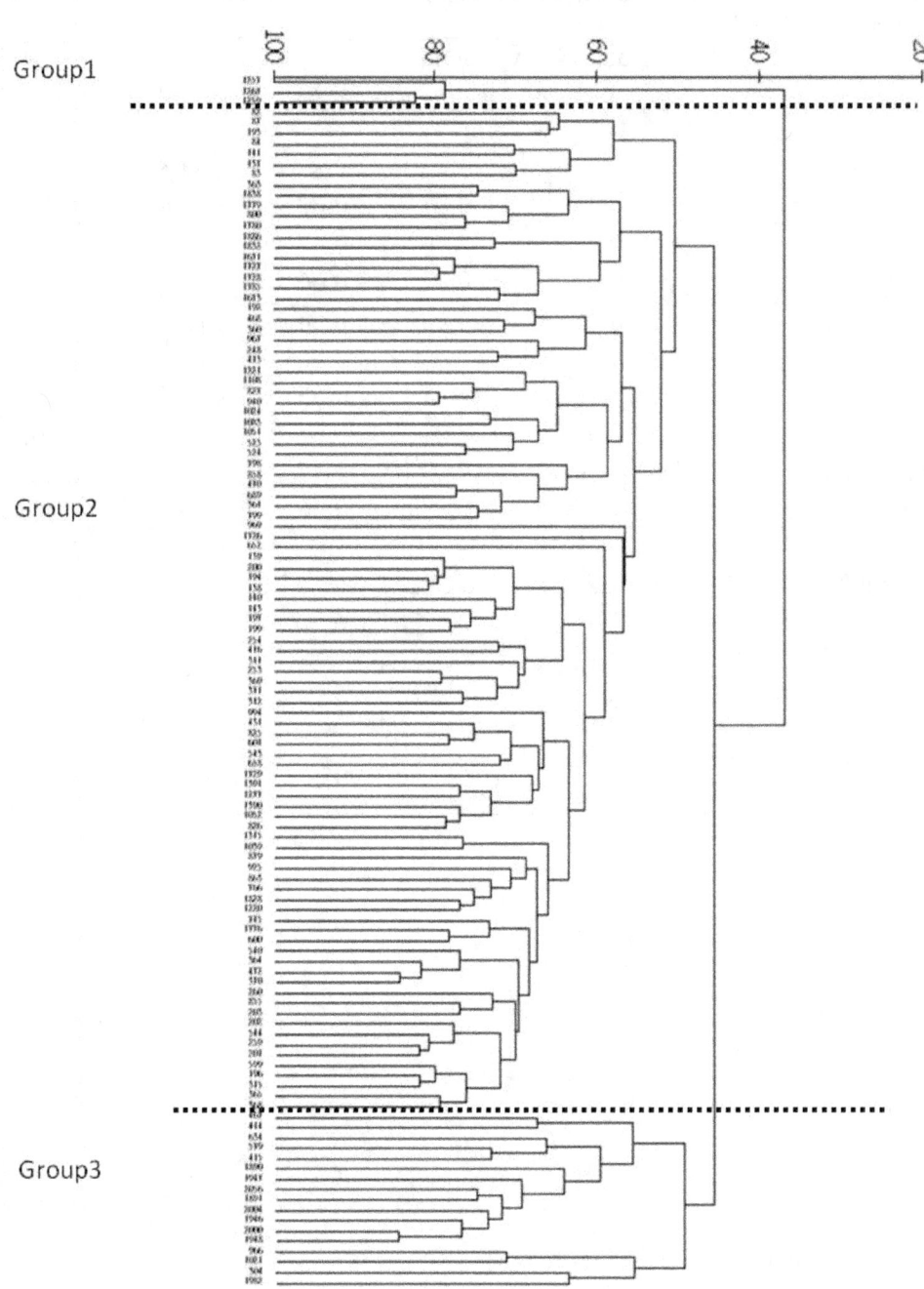

Figure 8A. Cluster analysis of species similarity among hotspots at the 10-km scale. Planning-units are clustered into three groups. Each number represents a grid cell identified as a hotspot (n=117).

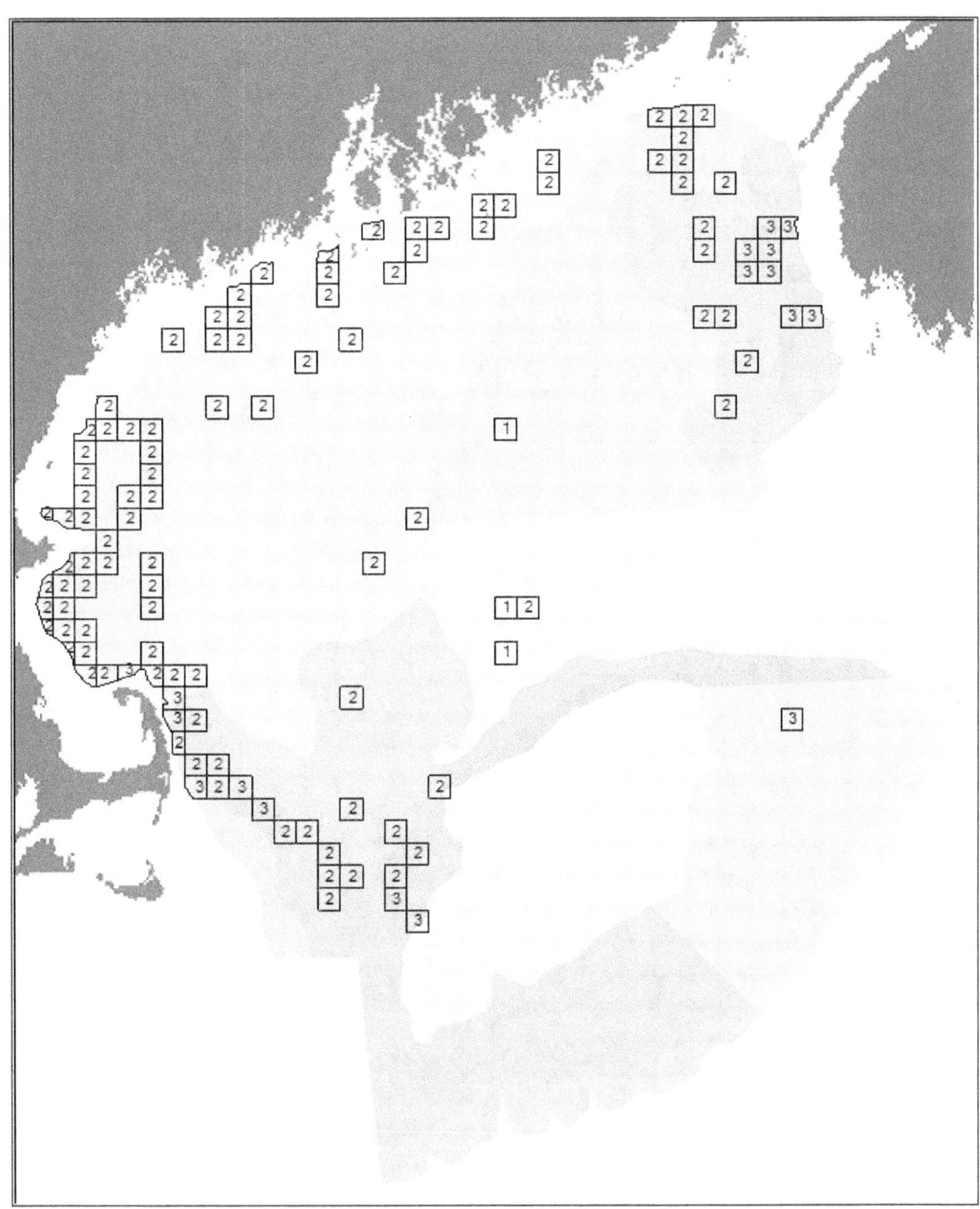

Figure 8B. Distribution of the three cluster groups at the 10-km scale.

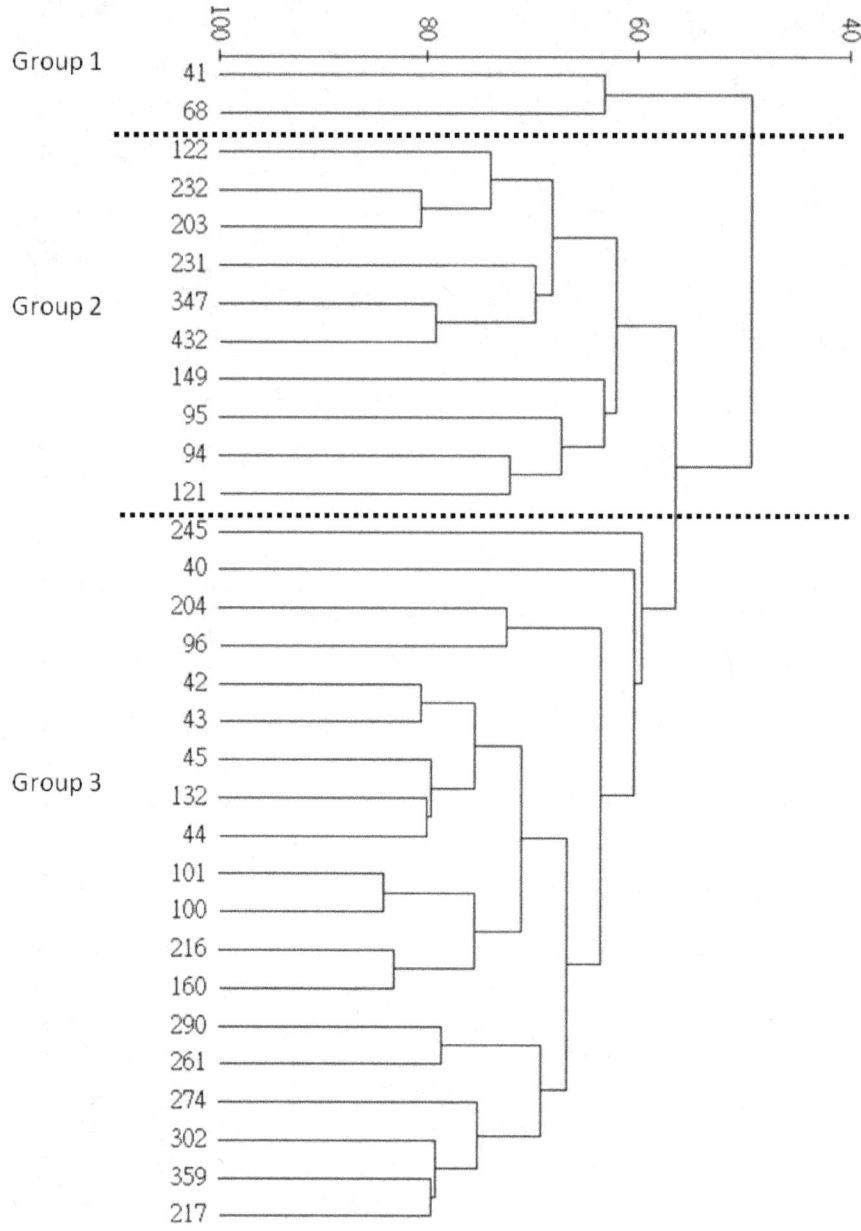

Figure 9A. Cluster analysis of species similarity among hotspots at the 20-km scale. Planning-units are clustered into three groups. Each number represents a grid cell identified as a hotspot (n=31).

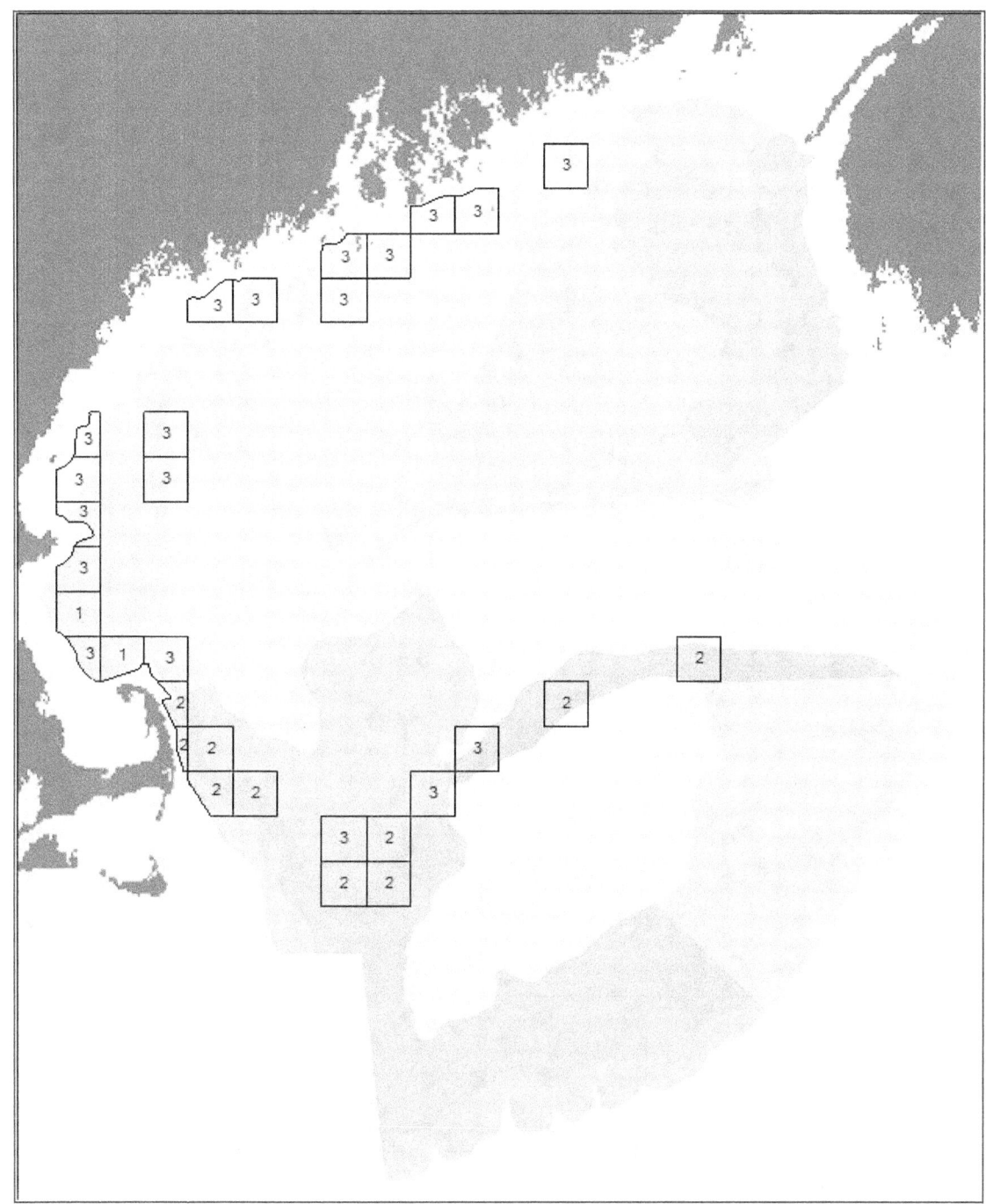

Figure 9B. Distribution of the three cluster groups at the 20-km scale.

Similarity

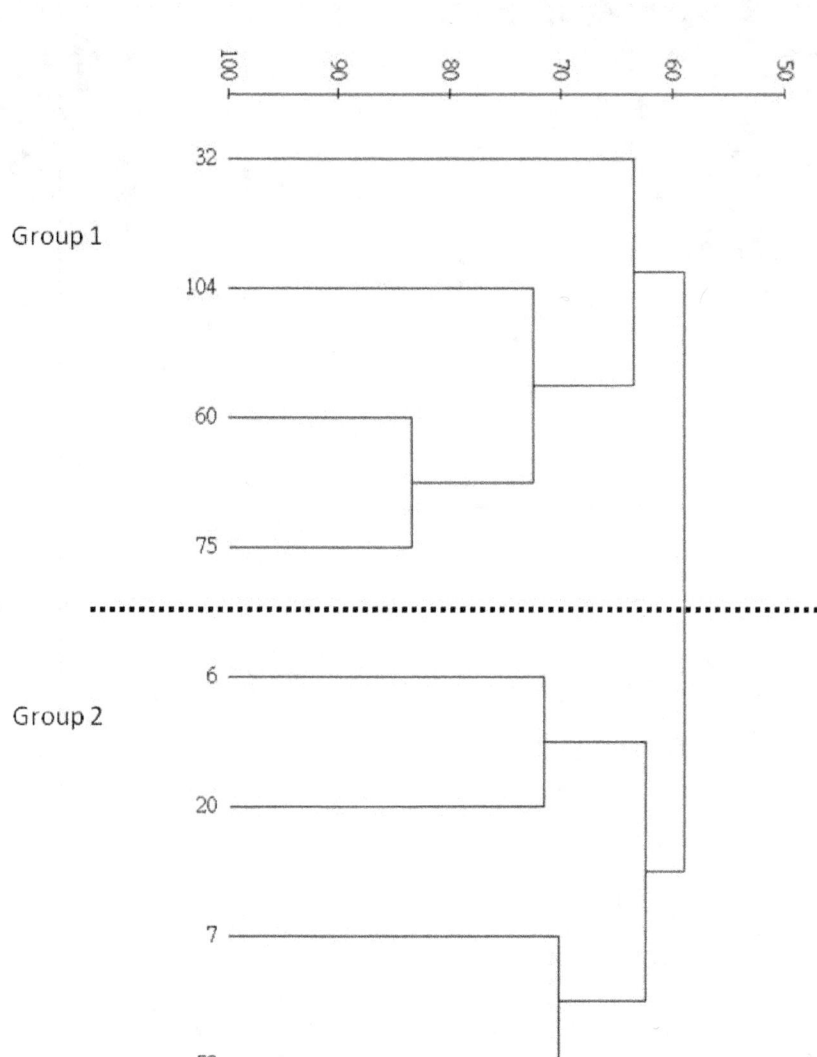

Figure 10A. Cluster analysis of species similarity among hotspots at the 40- km scale. Planning-units are clustered into three groups. Each number represents a grid cell identified as a hotspot (n=8).

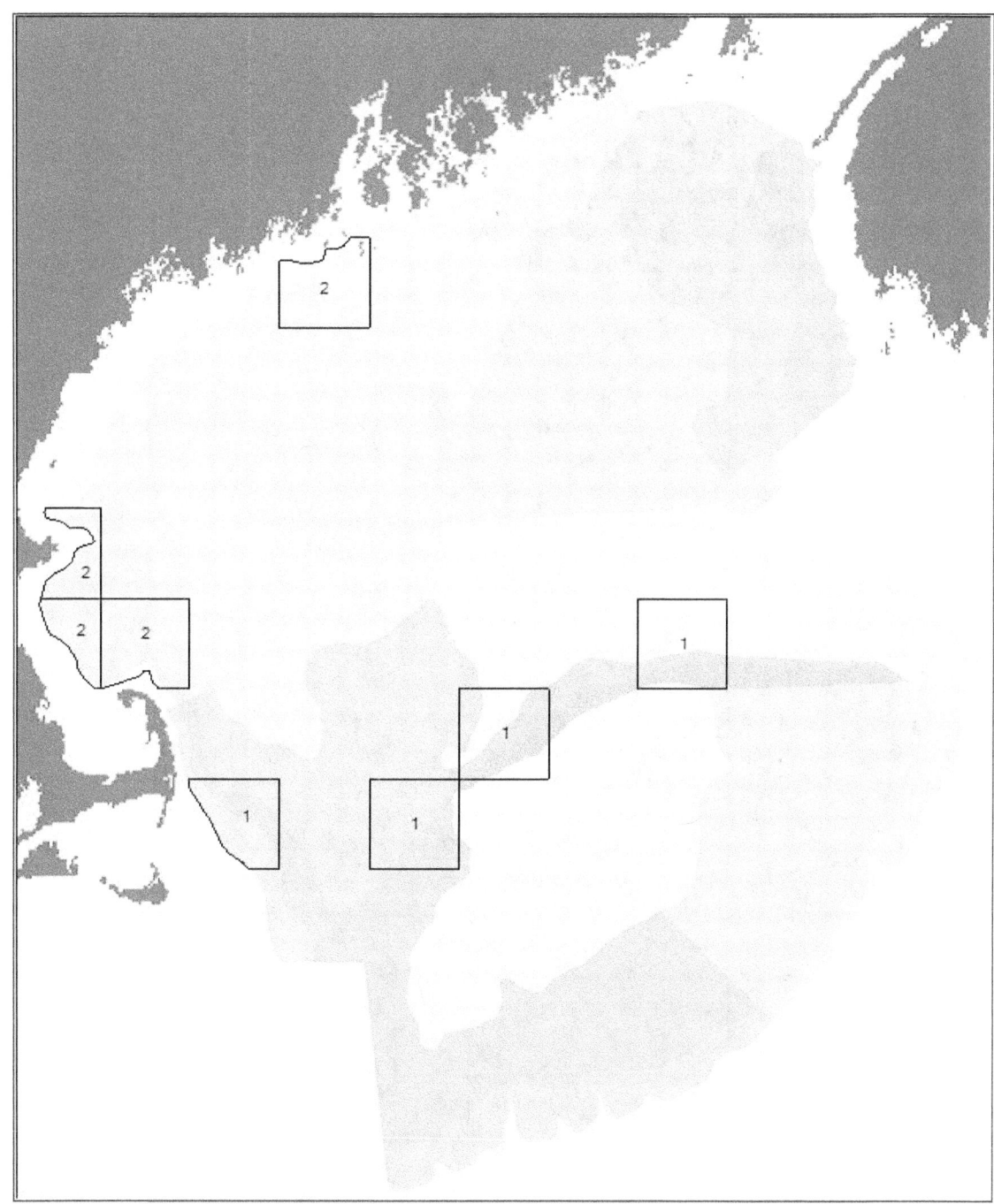

Figure 10B. Distribution of the two cluster groups at the 40-km scale.

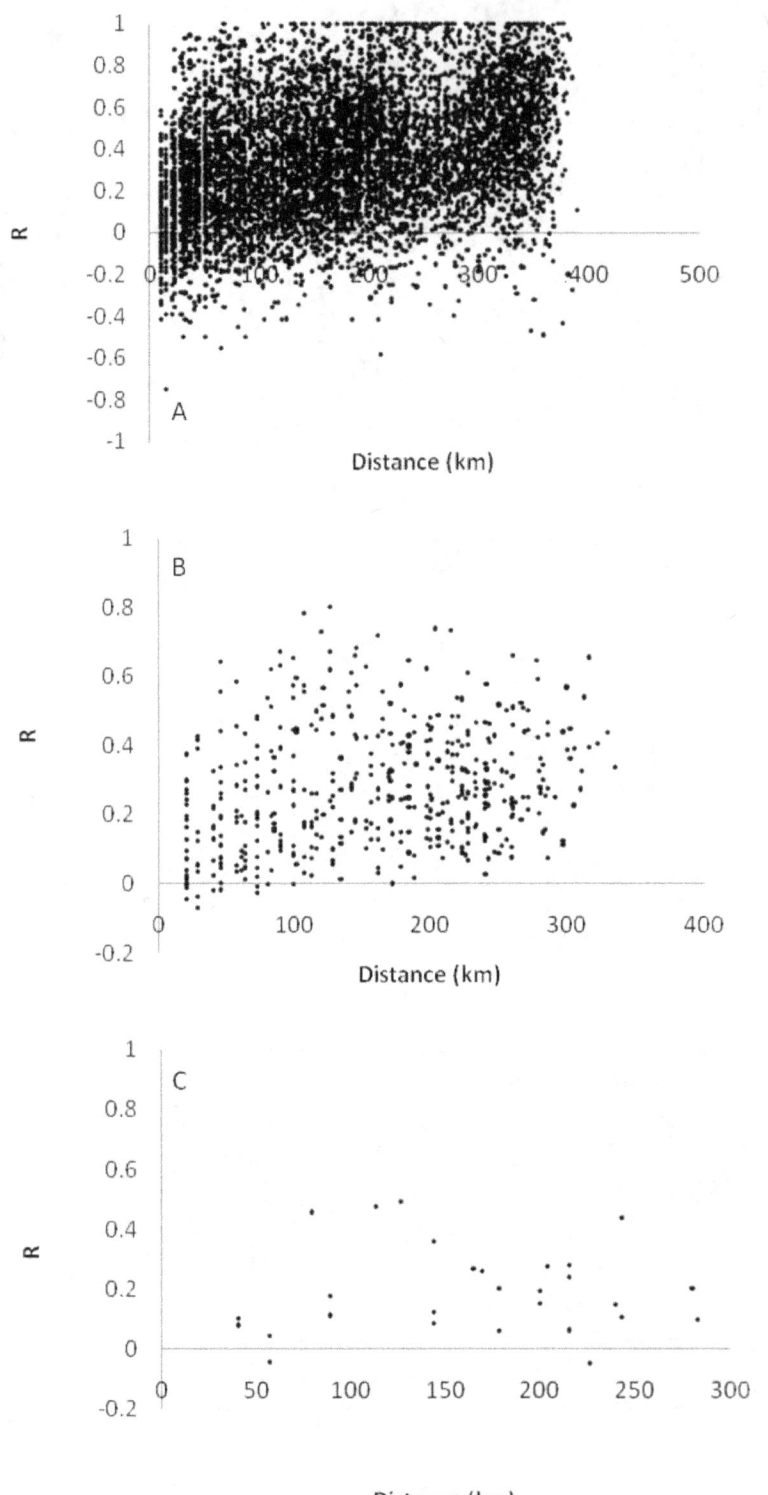

Figure 11. The relationship of dissimilarity (R value) and distance between hotspots at (A) 10-km scale (B) 20-km scale, and (C) 40-km scale.

Global R values from the ANOSIM conducted for all comparisons among hotspots were 0.349 (P<0.001) at the 10-km scale, 0.224 (P<0.001) at the 20-km scale, 0.183 at the 40-km (P<0.001) scale, and 0.021 (P=0.084) at the 80-km scale. The results demonstrated that the overall species similarity among hotspots increased when the spatial scale increased. If distance did significantly influence the degree of dissimilarity, we would expect a positive relationship between ANOSIM R value and distance. Regressions of ANOSIM R value versus distance between each hotspot pairs, at each planning-unit size, did not demonstrate any strong linear relationship (Figure 11). While regressions for the 10 km and 20 km scales were significant (p < 0.05), correlation coefficients were very low and slopes were close to zero. The regression at the 40 km scale was not significant (Table 11).

Discussion

Here we have demonstrated that planning-unit size and spatial variation in sampling effort can substantially influence emergent spatial patterns of diversity. Not surprisingly these results illustrated that total species richness was positively correlated with sample size. However, the smaller the sample size the greater the effect on the estimation of species richness tended to be as the regressions of sample size versus richness were steeper at small sample sizes in all cases. This pattern likely reflects the effect of small planning-units containing fewer samples with lower diversity than larger units resulting in an increased rate of species accumulation as sample size increased. Note that the slope value of the power curves decreased from 0.36 to 0.23 as planning-unit size increased from 10 km^2 to 80 km^2 and the Wilcox pair-wise comparison of regressions indicated that the slope value of the regression model at the 10-km scale was significantly higher than at larger planning-unit sizes. These results illustrated that the effect of sample size at small planning-unit sizes was significantly higher. With small planning-unit sizes, we suggest that small sample sizes are problematic for assessing spatial variation of species richness. Furthermore, about 50 % of hotspots changed regardless of planning-unit size when we compared the results from the estimation of total species richness and the effort-standardization approach. The number of unstable planning units was higher at finer scales (*e.g.*, 55 planning units at the 10-km scale) and such numbers may have problematic consequences in an MPA designation process.

Results demonstrate that use of the procedure to standardize effort represented in each planning unit addresses obvious problems inherent in use of the widely variable number of samples collected across the spatial extent of interest. Approaches for marine conservation planning vary, and how the data are used as a foundation for decision-making are sometimes ignored or at least not explicitly acknowledged. For example, the distribution of diversity is often used but variation in sampling effort and effects on diversity estimation and geographic pattern are not addressed (Andrew 2002). Hence, it is possible that we have identified hotspots in the past due in part to variation in sampling effort and missed some number of other sites that may have better met conservation goals or provided additional alternatives for consideration.

In this study, we present an initial investigation on the subject of the spatial patterns of species diversity in relation to planning-unit size in the Gulf of Maine. We used empirical data to reduce the effect of variation in sample size instead of other nonparametric techniques to predict species richness in each grid cell based on widely variable sample sizes. A robust and accurate estimator should be insensitive to sample size (Chazdon *et al.* 1998), however, multiple studies have demonstrated that sample size has a crucial effect on the nonparametric estimation on species richness (Andrew *et al.* 2003; Brose *et al.* 2003; Chazdon *et al.* 1998). Moreover, it is difficult to estimate the total number of species because there is always a high chance of excluding a large number of rare species (Bunge & Fitzpatrick 1993), especially if they have a clumped distribution.

Standardization approaches are needed to address variation of sample size within planning units in order to compare datasets (Gotelli & Colwell 2001). We re-sampled the empirical data by programming to overcome the issues of uneven sample size, thus each grid cell was comparable to all others. We randomly re-sampled tows 1000 times from the dataset in each of the grids and calculated average number of species represented by the re-sampled tows. Our procedure was similar to sample-based rarefaction (Gotelli & Colwell 2001), except that we re-sampled data from an empirical dataset and used mean values to represent the results. This procedure was designed to select hotspots, at least based on relative differences in species richness among planning units, rather than on estimation of predicted species richness. However, while the effort standardization approach can overcome the issues of large sample size resulting in overexpression of species richness, grid cells with small sample sizes still remain an issue as the procedure repetitively re-samples the same tows.

The locations of species-richness hotspots are used for many aspects of MPA design. The goal of many MPA designations is to conserve as many species as possible (Higgs & Usher 1980; McNeill & Fairweather 1993; Palmer *et al.* 1997; Roberts *et al.* 2003; Rowe and Sedberry 2006; Semmens et al. 2010). From an ecosystem management perspective, one of the most critical benefits of conserving species diversity is the redundancy that species provide within functional guilds and thus increase the resilience of ecosystems (Palmer *et al.* 1997; Sandin *et al.* 2008, Auster & Link 2009). In this study, patterns of species richness were clearly dependent on the spatial scale of planning-units and the location of hotspots changed across multiple spatial scales. The shifts in hotspot patterns may be due to the variation in the patchiness of habitats and attendant variation in the habitat affinities of the fish fauna (e.g., Auster 2002; Auster *et al.* 2001, 2006; Rosenzweig 1995). Increasing planning-unit sizes likely encompass more habitats and hence greater diversity of the fish fauna as diverse habitat-specific faunas merge (Rosenzweig 1995; Zagmajster *et al.* 2008). In particular, species-richness hotspots along the coast proportionally decreased and shifted to the complex topography along the edges of Georges Bank when planning-unit size increased. The habitats near the edge of Georges Bank are complex with high variation of bathymetry, sediment type, temperature, and circulation systems (Butman & Beardsley 1987).

Choices for threshold values to define hotspots can be rather arbitrary. Here we chose 10% based on use in a previous study but others have used different threshold values for hotspots (e.g., top quintile from each of six diversity indices in Auster *et al* 2006, top 5% in Lennon *et al.* 2001, top 15% in Zagmajster *et al.* 2008). We also mapped richness based on the distribution of quintiles and found similar trends in shifts in distribution based on planning unit size. From an applied perspective such maps are useful for assessing alternative protected area scenarios in terms of trade-offs of planning units in the top 10% of richness with other high diversity sites in the top quintile. The designation of MPAs, at least in the United States, is governed by a regulatory process that involves assessment of alternative strategies and a nested social process of negotiation. While hotspots may serve as set of ideal sites, alternative sites may ultimately be used due to overarching conflicts with various stakeholder interests.

Another issue related to MPA design is to decide how large sites should be. Some researchers suggest a number of small reserves protect more species than a single large reserve (Higgs & Usher 1980; McNeill & Fairweather 1993). In this study, the two hotspots identified at the 80-km scale included more species than the 117 hotspots identified at the 10-km scale. However, at the 10-km scale, the highest global R value and a higher proportion of pair-wise R values reached the value of one, indicating that species compositions were more dissimilar at finer planning-unit sizes. As discussed above, species distributions are demonstrably correlated with habitat features at these spatial scales (Auster *et al.* 1998; Langton and Watling, 1990) and small planning units generally contain fewer habitat types. If we take the total area of hotspots and species dissimilarity into account, it is possible that several small MPAs would protect more species than a single large MPA as there is a greater level of similarity at larger planning-unit sizes. Interestingly, distance was not a significant factor that affected species similarity between hotspots as there were no strong relationships based on distance between hotspots and species similarity at any planning-unit size.

We also found that there were more negative ANOSIM R values at the 10-km scale. R is a measure of variation between samples within grid cells compared to variation between grid cells (Clarke 1993). Theoretically, negative values are unlikely because they may represent greater dissimilarity among replicates within grid cells than between grid cells (Chapman & Underwood 1999). However, negative ANOSIM R values happened commonly in other studies and the phenomenon has been attributed either to inadequate sampling of species within delineated areas (*e.g.*, habitats) or inappropriate grouping of samples for analysis (Chapman & Underwood 1999). The higher proportion of negative ANOSIM R values in this study was more common at fine spatial scales and may be indicative such differences among planning units. For example, when sample size within planning units was small, less temporal variability was represented, thus the variation among samples from different years may be higher than the variation among planning units.

Many species that contributed most to dissimilarity between two groups of hotspots were relatively common at the scale of the NELME but may be linked to particular habitats or have restricted distributions at the scale of planning units. Hence small planning-unit size increases differences in species compositions and differences between groups. For example, cusk (*Brosme brosme*) had high contribution to the dissimilarity between hotspot groups at the 10-km and 20-km scale but not at the 40-km scale. Cusk occur primarily in boulder, ledge and gravel habitats (Auster & Lindholm 2005; Collette & Klein-MacPhee 2002) that are primarily limited to the upper slopes and peaks of offshore banks (except Georges Bank), coastal Maine, and the heads of submarine canyons. Hence, the contribution of cusk to the dissimilarity of hotspots will depend on inclusion of such habitats within planning units, with larger planning units having an increased probability of encompassing such features.

In this study we focused on patterns of species richness based on combining samples across the entire time series in the data set. Issues of sub-population structure, variation in use of multiple habitats, and temporal variation of community composition remain. However, sample size within individual planning units was minimal even with the aggregated data and temporal subsets of data would have been inadequate to support the analysis in most of the grid cells at fine planning-unit sizes. Although it is possible that several smaller MPAs can protect more species than a large MPA, we suggest that there would be more biased information from fine grid cells because of the effect of sample size and patchy distribution of fishes if we want to use empirical data for hotspot analysis. In other words, selecting hotspots from coarser spatial scale is less influenced by sample size and patchiness. Some studies indicate that larger protected areas with diverse habitats may maintain more stable conditions (Auster 2002; Hilborn *et al.* 2003). From a study in the Gulf of Maine region, species diversity declined at Stellwagen Bank National Marine Sanctuary (at a smaller scale) over time but has remained stable at the scale of the Gulf of Maine region overall (Auster 2002).

There is a great need for identifying proxies for predicting the distribution of biological diversity to aid in conservation planning (Ward *et al.* 1999), as surveys across broad taxonomic groups are time-consuming and costly. The distribution and abundance of fishes are well known in many areas with active fisheries and understanding their role as a proxy (*i.e.* based on single taxa, community structure, measures of diversity) would be useful in this regard (Auster et al. 2001; Cook & Auster 2006). However, there are few empirical tests to demonstrate such relationships. There is a degree of spatial concordance of geographic boundaries based of Georges Bank fish communities with benthic communities in the same region (Auster & Shackell 2000; Overholtz & Tyler 1985; Theroux & Grosslein 1987) but further study is needed to demonstrate the robustness of such correlations.

This study provides a foundation for marine conservation planning based on identification of diversity hotspots using geographically comprehensive data on demersal fishes, a type of data set common to regions and nations with developed commercial fisheries. The spatial extent of the region of interest is a critical decision to be made prior to any analyses. Here we addressed the region of the NELME. However, smaller or larger regions based on biogeographic patterns, oceanographic regimes, and habitat or landscapes of interests can be used to define the region of study (Cook & Auster 2007). Here we have demonstrated that larger planning-unit size reduces problems related to estimation of diversity and identification of hotspots. Given this result, identifying hotspots over larger regions may be useful as a first step and then subsequently investigating patterns of diversity within such planning units may lead to more strategically targeted MPA designs.

Acknowledgements

The authors gratefully acknowledge the support provided by the Taiwanese Ministry of Education (to CYK), the Census of Marine Life Gulf of Maine Program (to PA), and NOAA's National Undersea Research Program. Dr. Randal Clark of NOAA's National Centers for Coastal Ocean Science provided the data set used in this analysis. Drs. Eric Schultz and Daniel Civco provided many useful comments over the course of this project that greatly improved the final product. Drs. Ming-Hui Chen and Xia Wan provided important statistical advice. The authors also thanks three anonymous reviewers for comments that greatly improved the manuscript. The opinions expressed herein are those of the authors and do not necessarily reflect the opinions of the funding organizations or their sub-agencies.

Literature Cited

Allison, G. W., J. Lubchenco, and M. H. Carr. 1998. Marine reserves are necessary but not sufficient for marine conservation. Ecological Applications **8**:S79-S92.

Andrew, F., J. A. Martin, T. F. Matthew, and A. R. Ashley. 2003. Estimating marine species richness: an evaluation of six extrapolative techniques. Marine Ecology Progress Series **248**:15-26.

Andrew, R. G. P. 2002. Simultaneous 'hotspots' and 'coldspots' of marine biodiversity and implications for global conservation. Marine Ecology Progress Series **241**:23-27.

Arrhenius, O. 1921. Species and area. The Journal of Ecology **9**:95-99.

Auster, P. J. 2002. Representation of biological diversity of the Gulf of Maine region at Stellwagen Bank National Marine Sanctuary (Northwest Atlantic): patterns of fish diversity and assemblage composition. Pages 1096-1125 in S. Bondrup-Nielsen, N. W. P. Munro, G. Nelson, J. H. M. Willison, T. B. Herman, and P. Eagles, editors. Managing Protected Areas in a Changing World. SAMPAA, Wolfville, Canada.

Auster, P.J. and J. Link. 2009. Compensation and recovery of feeding guilds in a northwest Atlantic shelf fish community. Marine Ecology Progress Series 382:163–172.

Auster, P.J., K. Joy, and P.C. Valentine. 2001. Fish species and community distributions as proxies for seafloor habitat distributions: the Stellwagen Bank National Marine Sanctuary example (Northwest Atlantic, Gulf of Maine). Environmental Biology of Fishes 60:331-346.

Auster, P. J., R. Clark, and R. E. S. Reed. 2006. Marine fishes. Pages 89-229 in T. Bttista, R. Clark, and S. Pittman, editors. An Ecological Characterization of the Stellwagen Bank National Marine Sanctuary Region: Oceanographic, Biogeographic, and Contaminants Assessment. CCMA/NOAA/NOS/NCCOS, Silver Spring, MD.

Auster, P. J., K. Joy, and P. C. Valentine. 2001. Fish species and community distributions as proxies for seafloor habitat distributions: the Stellwagen Bank National Marine Sanctuary example (Northwest Atlantic, Gulf Of Maine). Environmental Biology of Fishes **60**:331-346.

Auster, P. J., and R. W. Langton, editors. 1999. The effects of fishing on fish habitat. *In* Fish Habitat: essential fish habitat and rehabilitation, pages 150-187. L. R. Benaka, editor. American Fisheries Society Symposium 22. Bethesda, Maryland, USA.

Auster, P. J., and J. Lindholm. 2005. The ecology of fishes on deep boulder reefs in the western Gulf of Maine. Pages 89-107. Diving for Science 2005, Proceedings of the American Academy of Underwater Sciences. Connecticut Sea Grant, Groton, CT.

Auster, P. J., C. Michalopoulos, P. C. Valentine, R. J. Malatesta. 1998. Delineating and monitoring habitat management units in a temperate deep-water marine protected area. Pages 169–185 in N. W. P. Munro J. H. M. Willison, editors. Linking protected areas with working landscapes, conserving biodiversity. Science and Management of Protected Areas Association, Wolfville , Nova Scotia .

Auster, P. J., and N. L. Shackell. 2000. Marine protected areas for the temperate and boreal northwest Atlantic: the potential for sustainable fisheries and conservation of biodiversity. Northeastern Naturalist **7**:419-434.

Azarovitz, T. R. 1981. A brief historical review of the Woods Hole Laboratory trawl survey time series. Pages 62-67 in W. Doubleday, and D. Rivard, editors. Bottom trawl surveys. Canadian Special Publication of Fisheries and Aquatic Sciences.

Bakus, R. H., and D. W. Bourne 1987. Georges Bank. The MIT Press, Cambridge, Massachusettts, USA.

Benjamin S. Halpern, R. R. W. 2002. Marine reserves have rapid and lasting effects. Ecology Letters **5**:361-366.

Bohning-Gaese, K. 1997. Determinants of avian species richness at different spatial scales. Journal of Biogeography **24**:49-60.

Botsford, L. W., F. Micheli, and A. Hastings. 2003. Principles for the design of marine reserves. Ecological Applications **13**:25-31.

Brose, U., N. D. Martinez, and R. J. Williams. 2003. Estimating species richness: sensitivity to sample coverage and insensitivity to spatial patterns. Ecology **84**:2364-2377.

Bunge, J., and M. Fitzpatrick. 1993. Estimating the Number of Species. Journal of the American Statistical Association **88**:364-373.

Butman, B., and R. C. Beardsley. 1987. Physical Oceanography. Pages 88-169 in B. Butman, S. B. Peterson, M. D. Grosslein, J. S. Schlee, P. Falkowski, J. M. Teal, D. R. Christie, and R. C. Beardsley, editors. Georges Bank. MIT Press, London, England.

Chapman, M. G., and A. J. Underwood. 1999. Ecological patterns in multivariate assemblages: information and interpretation of negative values in ANOSIM tests. Marine Ecology Progress Series **180**:257-265.

Chazdon, R. L., R. K. Colwell, J. S. Denslow, and M. R. Guariguata. 1998. Statistical methods for estimating species richness of woody regeneration in primary and secondary rain forest of northeastern Costa Rica. Pages 285-309 in F. Dallmeier, and J. A. Comiskey, editors. Forest biodiversity research, monitoring and modeling: conceptual background and old world case studies. UNESCO, Paris.

Clarke, K. R. 1993. Non-parametric multivariate analyses of changes in community structure. Austral Ecology **18**:117-143.

Clarke, K. R., and R. M. Warwick 2001. Change in Marine Communities: an Approach to Statistical Analysis and Interpretation. PRIMER-E Ltd, Plymouth, U.K.

Collette, B.B. and G. Klein-MacPhee (eds.). 2002. Bigelow and Schroeder's Fishes of the Gulf of Maine. Smithsonian Institution Press, Washington.

Collie, J. S., S. J. Hall, M. J. Kaiser, and I. R. Poiner. 2000. A quantitative analysis of fishing impacts on shelf-sea benthos. The Journal of Animal Ecology **69**:785-798.

Connor, E. F., and E. D. McCoy. 1979. The statistics and biology of the species-area relationship. The American Naturalist **113**:791-833.

Cook, R.R. and P.J. Auster. 2007. A bioregional classification of the continental shelf of northeastern North America for conservation analysis and planning based on representation. Marine Sanctuaries Conservation Series NMSP-07-03. U.S. Department of Commerce, National Oceanic and Atmospheric Administration, National Marine Sanctuary Program, Silver Spring, MD.

Cook, R.R. and P.J. Auster. 2006. Developing alternatives for optimal representation of seafloor habitats and associated communities in Stellwagen Bank National Marine Sanctuary. Marine Sanctuaries Conservation Series ONMS-06-02. U.S. Department of

Commerce, National Oceanic and Atmospheric Administration, National Marine
Sanctuary Program, Silver Spring, MD.

Friedlander, A. M. 2001. Essential fish habitat and the effective design of narine reserves:
application for marine ornamental fishes. Aquarium Sciences and Conservation 3:135-
150.

Garrison, L. P., and J. S. Link. 2000. Fishing effects on spatial distribution and trophic
guild structure of the fish community in the Georges Bank region. ICES J. Mar. Sci.
57:723-730.

Gell, F. R., and C. M. Roberts. 2003. Benefits beyond boundaries: the fishery effects of
marine reserves. Trends in Ecology & Evolution **18**:448-455.

Gotelli, N. J., and R. K. Colwell. 2001. Quantifying biodiversity: procedures and pitfalls
in the measurement and comparison of species richness. Ecology Letters **4**:379-391.

Grosslein, M. D. 1979. Groundfish survey program of BCF Woods Hole. Commercial
Fisheries Review **31**:22-30.

Halpern, B. S. 2003. The impact of marine reserves: do reserves work and does reserve
size matter? Ecological Applications **13**:117-137.

Halpern, B. S., and R. R. Warner. 2002. Marine reserves have rapid and lasting effects.
Ecology Letters **5**:361-366.

Halpern, B. S., and R. R. Warner. 2003. Matching marine reserve design to reserve
objectives. Proceedings of the Royal Society B: Biological Sciences **270**:1871-1878.

Higgs, A. J., and M. B. Usher. 1980. Should nature reserves be large or small? Nature
285:568-569.

Hilborn, R., T. P. Quinn, D. E. Schindler, and D. E. Rogers. 2003. Biocomplexity and
fisheries sustainability. Proceedings of the National Academy of Sciences of the United
States of America **100**:6564-6568.

Langton, R.; Watling, L. 1990. The fish-benthos connection: a definition of prey groups
in the Gulf of Maine. *In* Trophic Relationships in the Marine Environment: Proceedings
of the 24th European Marine Biology Symposium, pages 424-238. M. Barnes and R. N.
Gibson, editors. European Marine Biology Symposia.

Lennon, J. J., P. Koleff, J. J. D. Greenwood, and K. J. Gaston. 2001. The geographical
structure of British bird distributions: diversity, spatial turnover and scale. Journal of
Animal Ecology **70**:966-979.

Lindholm, J., P. Auster, and P. Valentine. 2004. Role of a large marine protected area for conserving landscape attributes of sand habitats on Georges Bank (NW Atlantic). Marine Ecology Progress Series **269**:61-68.

Lindholm, J. B., P. J. Auster, M. Ruth, and L. Kaufman. 2001. Modeling the effects of fishing and implications for the design of marine protected Areas: juvenile fish responses to variations in seafloor habitat. The Journal of the Society for Conservation Biology **15**:424-437.

Link, J. S. 2005. Translating ecosystem indicators into decision criteria. ICES J. Mar. Sci. **62**:569-576.

McNeill, S. E., and P. G. Fairweather. 1993. Single large or several small marine reserves? An experimental approach with seagrass fauna. Journal of Biogeography **20**:429-440.

Mora, C., S. Andrefouet, M. J. Costello, C. Kranenburg, A. Rollo, J. Veron, K. J. Gaston, and R. A. Myers. 2006. Coral reefs and the global network of marine protected areas. Science **312**:1750-1751.

Mumby, P. J., C. P. Dahlgren, A. R. Harborne, C. V. Kappel, F. Micheli, D. R. Brumbaugh, K. E. Holmes, J. M. Mendes, K. Broad, J. N. Sanchirico, K. Buch, S. Box, R. W. Stoffle, and A. B. Gill. 2006. Fishing, trophic cascades, and the process of grazing on coral reefs. Science **311**:98-101.

Murawski, S. A., S. E. Wigley, M. J. Fogarty, P. J. Rago, and D. G. Mountain. 2005. Effort distribution and catch patterns adjacent to temperate MPAs. ICES J. Mar. Sci. **62**:1150-1167.

Myers, N., R. A. Mittermeier, C. G. Mittermeier, G. A. B. da Fonseca, and J. Kent. 2000. Biodiversity hotspots for conservation priorities. Nature **403**:853-858.

NOAA National Centers for Coastal Ocean Science (NCCOS) 2006. An Ecological Characterization of the Stellwagen Bank National Marine Sanctuary Region: Oceanographic, Biogeographic, and Contaminants Assessment. Prepared by NCCOS's Biogeography Team in cooperation with the National Marine Sanctuary Program. Silver Spring, MD. NOAA Technical Memorandum NOS NCCOS 45.

NEFSC. 1988. An evaluation of the bottom trawl survey program of the northeast fisheries center. 83 pp. National Marine Fisheries Service. NOAA Technical Memo, NMFS-F/NEC-52.

Overholtz, W. J., and A. V. Tyler. 1985. Long-term responses of the dermersal fish assemblages of Georges Bank. United States Fisheries Bulletin **83: 507-520**.

Palmer, M. A., R. F. Ambrose, and N. L. Poff. 1997. Ecological theory and community restoration ecology. Restoration Ecology **5**:291-300.

Palmer, M. W., and P. S. White. 1994. Scale dependence and the species-area relationship. The American Naturalist **144**:717.

Quinn, G. P., and M. J. Keough 2003. Experimental Design and Data Analysis for Biologists. Cambridge University Press, Cambridge, United Kingdom.

Rahbek, C. 2005. The role of spatial scale and the perception of large-scale species-richness patterns. Ecology Letters **8**:224-239.

Reid, W. V. 1998. Biodiversity hotspots. Trends in Ecology & Evolution **13**:275-280.

Roberts, C. M., G. Branch, R. H. Bustamante, J. C. Castilla, J. Dugan, B. S. Halpern, K. D. Lafferty, H. Leslie, J. Lubchenco, D. McArdle, M. Ruckelshaus, and R. R. Warner. 2003. Application of ecological criteria in selecting marine reserves and developing reserve networks. Ecological Applications **13**:215-228.

Rosenzweig, M. L. 1995. Species Diversity in Space and Time. Cambrige University Press, Cambridge.

Rowe, J.J., and G.R. Sedberry. 2006. Integrating GIS with fishery survey historical data: a possible tool for designing marine protected areas. Proceedings of the Gulf and Caribbean Fisheries Institute **57**:9-30.

Sandin, S. A., J. E. Smith, E. E. DeMartini, E. A. Dinsdale, S. D. Donner, A. M. Friedlander, T. Konotchick, M. Malay, J. E. Maragos, D. Obura, O. Pantos, G. Paulay, M. Richie, F. Rohwer, R. E. Schroeder, S. Walsh, J. B. C. Jackson, N. Knowlton, and E. Sala. 2008. Baselines and degradation of coral reefs in the northern Line Islands. PLoS ONE **3**:e1548.

Semmens, B.X., P.J. Auster and M.J. Paddack. 2010. Using ecological null models to assess the potential for marine protected area networks to protect biodiversity. PLoS ONE **5**: e8895.

Sherman, K., N. A. Jaworski, and T. J. Smayda 1996. The northeast shelf ecosystem: assessment, sustainability, and management. Blackwell Science, Cambridge, Mass. (USA).

Theroux, R. B., and M. D. Grosslein. 1987. Benthic fauna. Pages 283-295 in R. H. Backus, and D. Bourne, editors. Georges Bank. MIT Press, Cambridge, MA, USA.

Ward, T. J., M. A. Vanderklift, A. O. Nicholls, and R. A. Kenchington. 1999. Selecting marine reserves using habitats and species assemblages as surrogates for biological diversity. Ecological Applications **9**:691-698.

William, D. N. 1986. Species-area relationship and its determinants for mammals in western North American national parks. Biological Journal of the Linnaean Society **28**:83-98.

Willis, K. J., and R. J. Whittaker. 2002. Species diversity--scale matters. Science **295**:1245-1248.

Zagmajster, M., D. C. Culver, and B. Sket. 2008. Species richness patterns of obligate subterranean beetles (Insecta: Coleoptera) in a global biodiversity hotspot; effect of scale and sampling intensity. Diversity and Distributions **14**:95-105.

Appendix 1. List of scientific and common names of fishes captured in spring and fall NMFS trawl samples within the NELME, 1975-2005.

Scientific name	Common name
Alosa aestivalis	blueback herring
Alosa mediocris	hickory shad
Alosa pseudoharengus	Alewife
Alosa sapidissima	American shad
Aluterus schoepfi	orange filefish
Amblyraja radiata	thorny skate
Ammodytes americanus	American sand lance
Ammodytes dubius	northern sand lance
Anarhichas lupus	Atlantic wolfish
Anchoa hepsetus	striped anchovy
Anchoa mitchilli	bay anchovy
Anguilla rostrata	american eel
Antennarius radiosus	singlespot frogfish
Antigonia capros	deepbody boarfish
Antimora rostrata	blue hake
Apeltes quadracus	fourspine stickleback
Archosargus probatocephalus	sheepshead
Arctozenus rissoi	white barracudina
Argentina silus	Atlantic argentine
Argentina striata	striated argentine
Argyropelecus aculeatus	silver hatchetfish
Ariomma bondi	silver rag
Artediellus sp	hookear sculpin
Aspidophoroides monopterygius	alligatorfish
Balistes capriscus	gray triggerfish
Brevoortia tyrannus	Atlantic menhaden
Brosme brosme	cusk
Caranx crysos	blue runner
Centropristis ocyurus	bank sea bass
Centropristis striata	black sea bass
Ceratoscopelus maderensis	horned lanternfish
Chauliodus sloani	viperfish
Chaunax stigmaeus	redeye gaper
Chlorophthalmus agassizi	shortnose greeneye
Citharichthys arctifrons	gulf stream flounder
Clupea harengus	Atlantic herring
Coelorhynchus carminatus	long-nosed grenadier

Scientific name	Common name
Conger oceanicus	conger eel
Cookeolus japonicus	bulleye
Cryptacanthodes maculatus	wrymouth
Cubiceps pauciradiatus	bigeye cigarfish
Cyclopterus lumpus	lumpfish
Dactylopterus volitans	flying gurnard
Decapterus macarellus	mackerel scad
Decapterus punctatus	round scad
Dipturus laevis	barndoor skate
Enchelyopus cimbrius	fourbeard rockling
Engraulis eurystole	silver anchovy
Epigonus pandionis	bigeye
Etropus microstomus	smallmouth flounder
Etrumeus teres	round herring
Eumicrotremus spinosus	Atlantic spiny lumpsucker
Fistularia petimba	red cornetfish
Fistularia tabacaria	bluespotted cornetfish
Foetorepus agassizi	spotfin dragonet
Gadus morhua	Atlantic cod
Gasterosteus aculeatus	threespine stickleback
Glyptocephalus cynoglossus	witch flounder
Helicolenus dactylopterus	blackbelly rosefish
Hemitripterus americanus	sea raven
Hippoglossoides platessoides	american plaice
Hippoglossus hippoglossus	Atlantic halibut
Hyperoglyphe perciformis	barrelfish
Hyporhamphus unifasciatus	silverstripe halfbeak
Laemonema barbatulum	shortbeard codling
Lepophidium profundorum	fawn cusk-eel
Leucoraja erinacea	little skate
Leucoraja garmani	rosette skate
Leucoraja ocellata	winter skate
Limanda ferruginea	yellowtail flounder
Liparis atlanticus	Atlantic seasnail
Liparis inquilinus	inquiline snailfish
Lophius americanus	goosefish
Lopholatilus chamaeleonticeps	blue tilefish
Lumpenus lumpretaeformis	snakeblenny
Lumpenus maculatus	daubed shanny

Scientific name	Common name
Lycenchelys verrilli	wolf eelpout
Macrorhamphosus scolopax	longspine snipefish
Macrourus berglax	roughhead grenadier
Macrozoarces americanus	ocean pout
Malacocephalus occidentalis	western softhead grenadier
Malacoraja senta	smooth skate
Mallotus villosus	capelin
Maurolicus weitzmani	weitzmans pearlsides
Melanogrammus aeglefinus	haddock
Melanostigma atlanticum	Atlantic soft pout
Menidia menidia	Atlantic silverside
Merluccius albidus	offshore hake
Merluccius bilinearis	silver hake
Monacanthus hispidus	planehead filefish
Monolene sessilicauda	deepwater flounder
Morone saxatilis	striped bass
Mustelus canis	smooth dogfish
Myctophum humboldti	humboldts lanternfish
Myoxocephalus aenaeus	grubby
Myoxocephalus octodecemspinosus	longhorn sculpin
Myoxocephalus scorpius	shorthorn sculpin
Myxine glutinosa	Atlantic hagfish
Naucrates ductor	pilotfish
Nemichthys scolopaceus	slender snipe eel
Nezumia bairdi	marlin-spike
Ogcocephalus corniger	longnose batfish
Ogcocephalus nasutus	shortnose batfish
Ophichthus cruentifer	margined snake eel
Ophidion selenops	mooneye cusk-eel
Opsanus tau	oyster toadfish
Orthopristis chrysoptera	pigfish
Osmerus mordax	rainbow smelt
Paralepis coregonoides	sharpchin barracudina
Paralichthys dentatus	summer flounder
Paralichthys oblongus	fourspot flounder
Parasudis truculenta	longnose greeneye
Peprilus triacanthus	butterfish
Peristedion miniatum	armored searobin
Petromyzon marinus	sea lamprey

Scientific name	Common name
Pholis gunnellus	rock gunnel
Pollachius virens	pollock
Polyipnus clarus	slope hatchetfish
Polymetme thaeocoryla	lightfish
Pomatomus saltatrix	bluefish
Priacanthus arenatus	bigeye
Prionotus carolinus	northern searobin
Pristigenys alta	short bigeye
Pseudopleuronectes americanus	winter flounder
Reinhardtius hippoglossoides	greenland halibut
Rhomboplites aurorubens	vermilion snapper
Sarda sarda	Atlantic bonito
Scomber japonicus	chub mackerel
Scomber scombrus	Atlantic mackerel
Scomberesox saurus	Atlantic saury
Scophthalmus aquosus	windowpane
Scyliorhinus retifer	chain dogfish
Sebastes fasciatus	acadian redfish
Selar crumenophthalmus	bigeye scad
Selene setapinnis	Atlantic moonfish
Selene vomer	lookdown
Seriola zonata	banded rudderfish
Simenchelys parasiticus	snubnose eel
Sphoeroides maculatus	northern puffer
Squalus acanthias	spiny dogfish
Stenotomus chrysops	scup
Stomias boa	scaly dragonfish
Symphurus civitatus	offshore tonguefish
Symphurus diomedianus	spottedfin tonguefish
Symphurus plagiusa	blackcheek tonguefish
Syngnathus fuscus	northern pipefish
Tautoga onitis	tautog
Tautogolabrus adspersus	cunner
Torpedo nobiliana	Atlantic torpedo
Trachurus lathami	rough scad
Trichiurus lepturus	Atlantic cutlassfish
Triglops murrayi	moustache sculpin
Ulvaria subbifurcata	radiated shanny
Urophycis chesteri	longfin hake

Scientific name	Common name
Urophycis chuss	red hake
Urophycis regia	spotted hake
Urophycis tenuis	white hake
Zenopsis conchifera	buckler dory

Appendix 2. Results of the curve estimation procedure on the relationship between sample size and species richness at 10-km scale.

Equation	Model Summary					Parameter Estimates	
	R Square	F	df1	df2	Sig.	Constant	b1
Linear	.830	107.541	1	22	.000	16.744	.872
Logarithmic	.934	311.951	1	22	.000	8.682	8.378
Power	.963	567.325	1	22	.000	11.608	.364
Growth	.739	62.146	1	22	.000	2.837	.035
Exponential	.739	62.146	1	22	.000	17.059	.035
Logistic	.739	62.146	1	22	.000	.059	.965

Appendix 3. Results of the curve estimation procedure on the relationship between sample size and species richness at 20-km scale.

Equation	Model Summary					Parameter Estimates	
	R Square	F	df1	df2	Sig.	Constant	b1
Linear	.830	107.541	1	22	.000	16.744	.872
Logarithmic	.934	311.951	1	22	.000	8.682	8.378
Power	.963	567.325	1	22	.000	11.608	.364
Growth	.739	62.146	1	22	.000	2.837	.035
Exponential	.739	62.146	1	22	.000	17.059	.035
Logistic	.739	62.146	1	22	.000	.059	.965

Appendix 4. Results of the curve estimation procedure on the relationship between sample size and species richness at 40-km scale.

Equation	Model Summary					Parameter Estimates	
	R Square	F	df1	df2	Sig.	Constant	b1
Linear	.720	164.778	1	64	.000	28.742	.194
Logarithmic	.757	199.013	1	64	.000	7.372	8.986
Power	.832	317.815	1	64	.000	15.250	.252
Growth	.654	121.070	1	64	.000	3.363	.005
Exponential	.654	121.070	1	64	.000	28.882	.005
Logistic	.654	121.070	1	64	.000	.035	.995

Appendix 5. Results of the curve estimation procedure on the relationship between sample size and species richness at 80-km scale.

Equation	Model Summary					Parameter Estimates	
	R Square	F	df1	df2	Sig.	Constant	b1
Linear	.675	53.882	1	26	.000	37.535	.080
Logarithmic	.764	84.372	1	26	.000	5.080	10.295
Power	.857	156.084	1	26	.000	16.718	.234
Growth	.616	41.783	1	26	.000	3.599	.002
Exponential	.616	41.783	1	26	.000	36.579	.002
Logistic	.616	41.783	1	26	.000	.027	.998

Appendix 6. SIMPER results for comparison of hotspot group 2 versus hotspot group 1 at 10-km spatial scale. Twenty-seven species contributed to 80 % of dissimilarity.

Species	Av.Abund Group 2	Av.Abund Group 1	Av.Diss	Diss/SD	Contrib%	Cum.%
Helicolenus dactylopterus	0.06	1.02	1.74	3.29	5.42	5.42
Argentina silus	0.05	0.57	1.73	3.28	5.4	10.82
Myoxocephalus octodecemspinosus	10.96	0	1.72	3.3	5.35	16.18
Pseudopleuronectes americanus	2.56	0	1.45	1.84	4.51	20.69
Limanda ferruginea	3.48	0	1.17	1.34	3.64	24.32
Artediellus sp	0.24	0.37	1.08	1.15	3.37	27.69
Brosme brosme	0.24	0.59	1.08	1.15	3.36	31.05
Enchelyopus cimbrius	1.69	0.11	1.07	1.15	3.32	34.37
Alosa sapidissima	0.3	0	1.02	1.1	3.18	37.56
Alosa aestivalis	2.11	0.07	1	1.06	3.11	40.67
Aspidophoroides monopterygius	0.5	0	0.97	1.06	3.03	43.69
Scomber scombrus	1.69	0.18	0.97	1.02	3.01	46.71
Myxine glutinosa	0.22	0.2	0.92	0.98	2.87	49.58
Peprilus triacanthus	0.98	0.44	0.9	0.94	2.8	52.38
Lumpenus maculatus	1.92	0.53	0.88	0.95	2.74	55.12
Anarhichas lupus	0.5	0.18	0.86	0.89	2.68	57.8
Paralichthys oblongus	0.46	0	0.82	0.9	2.55	60.35
Hippoglossus hippoglossus	0.12	0.07	0.78	0.86	2.43	62.78
Malacoraja senta	0.82	0.67	0.77	0.8	2.41	65.19
Leucoraja erinacea	0.96	0	0.71	0.79	2.2	67.39
Hemitripterus americanus	2.13	0.51	0.7	0.73	2.19	69.59
Leucoraja ocellata	0.55	0	0.7	0.79	2.17	71.76
Cyclopterus lumpus	0.1	0	0.67	0.74	2.1	73.86
Lycenchelys verrilli	0.02	0.07	0.63	0.75	1.98	75.83
Triglops murrayi	0.62	0	0.59	0.7	1.84	77.67
Argentina striata	0	0.2	0.58	0.71	1.8	79.47
Lumpenus lumpretaeformis	0.46	0	0.57	0.68	1.77	81.24

Appendix 7. SIMPER results for comparison of hotspot group 2 versus hotspot group 3 at 10-km spatial scale. Thirty-six species contributed to 80 % dissimilarity.

Species	AV.Abund Group2	Av.Abund Group3	Av.Diss	Diss/SD	Contrib%	Cum.%
Enchelyopus cimbrius	1.69	0	1.25	1.62	3.89	3.89
Malacoraja senta	0.82	0.07	1.12	1.28	3.49	7.38
Leucoraja erinacea	0.96	6.66	1.02	1.13	3.15	10.53
Leucoraja ocellata	0.55	7.52	1.01	1.13	3.15	13.68
Alosa aestivalis	2.11	0.25	0.98	1.13	3.05	16.73
Alosa sapidissima	0.3	0.04	0.94	1.08	2.92	19.65
Triglops murrayi	0.62	2.29	0.93	1.05	2.9	22.55
Scomber scombrus	1.69	2.07	0.91	1.01	2.82	25.37
Hippoglossus hippoglossus	0.12	0.27	0.89	1.01	2.78	28.15
Ammodytes dubius	3.01	1.69	0.89	1.01	2.76	30.91
Aspidophoroides monopterygius	0.5	0.91	0.85	0.94	2.65	33.56
Myxine glutinosa	0.22	0.03	0.85	0.98	2.65	36.21
Paralichthys oblongus	0.46	0.74	0.85	0.97	2.65	38.86
Sebastes fasciatus	33.73	0.75	0.84	0.94	2.6	41.47
Peprilus triacanthus	0.98	21.63	0.83	0.92	2.58	44.04
Scophthalmus aquosus	0.19	3.72	0.81	0.92	2.51	46.56
Brosme brosme	0.24	0.06	0.79	0.89	2.46	49.01
Lumpenus maculatus	1.92	0	0.75	0.88	2.33	51.34
Cyclopterus lumpus	0.1	0.05	0.74	0.85	2.31	53.65
Tautogolabrus adspersus	0.15	0.67	0.73	0.84	2.25	55.91
Anarhichas lupus	0.5	0.77	0.69	0.78	2.15	58.06
Limanda ferruginea	3.48	8.47	0.68	0.76	2.12	60.18
Glyptocephalus cynoglossus	6.32	0.72	0.68	0.76	2.12	62.3
Artediellus sp	0.24	0.08	0.67	0.77	2.07	64.37
Ulvaria subbifurcata	1.52	0.02	0.54	0.68	1.69	66.06
Lumpenus lumpretaeformis	0.46	0	0.53	0.68	1.66	67.71
Cryptacanthodes maculatus	0.11	0	0.5	0.65	1.54	69.25
Maurolicus weitzmani	0.11	0.15	0.48	0.62	1.5	70.75
Argentina silus	0.05	0.15	0.48	0.61	1.48	72.23
Prionotus carolinus	0.02	1.44	0.44	0.59	1.37	73.59
Myoxocephalus aenaeus	0.03	0.06	0.43	0.58	1.34	74.94
Pseudopleuronectes americanus	2.56	23.76	0.4	0.52	1.23	76.17
Dipturus laevis	0.02	0.06	0.39	0.54	1.22	77.39
Lophius americanus	0.97	0.35	0.39	0.5	1.2	78.59
Alosa pseudoharengus	9.67	2.47	0.37	0.49	1.16	79.75
Amblyraja radiata	2.37	2.07	0.36	0.48	1.11	80.86

Appendix 8. SIMPER results for comparison of hotspot group 3 versus hotspot group 1 at the 10-km spatial scale. Twenty-nine species contributed to 80 % dissimilarity.

Species	Av.Abund Group3	Av.Abund Group1	Av.Diss	Diss/SD	Contrib%	Cum.%
Pseudopleuronectes americanus	23.76	0	1.94	8.55	4.99	4.99
Myoxocephalus octodecemspinosus	35.65	0	1.94	8.55	4.99	9.97
Helicolenus dactylopterus	0.04	1.02	1.82	3.56	4.69	14.66
Limanda ferruginea	8.47	0	1.81	3.58	4.66	19.32
Leucoraja erinacea	6.66	0	1.6	2.06	4.11	23.43
Brosme brosme	0.06	0.59	1.6	2.06	4.1	27.54
Aspidophoroides monopterygius	0.91	0	1.58	2.07	4.07	31.61
Leucoraja ocellata	7.52	0	1.57	2.07	4.03	35.64
Argentina silus	0.15	0.57	1.49	1.73	3.83	39.47
Triglops murrayi	2.29	0	1.14	1.16	2.92	42.39
Artediellus sp	0.08	0.37	1.13	1.16	2.91	45.3
Malacoraja senta	0.07	0.67	1.09	1.13	2.8	48.11
Ammodytes dubius	1.69	0	1	1.03	2.58	50.69
Hippoglossus hippoglossus	0.27	0.07	0.99	1	2.54	53.22
Sebastes fasciatus	0.75	1.23	0.92	0.92	2.36	55.59
Scomber scombrus	2.07	0.18	0.9	0.89	2.3	57.89
Scophthalmus aquosus	3.72	0	0.8	0.82	2.05	59.94
Peprilus triacanthus	21.63	0.44	0.78	0.82	2	61.94
Anarhichas lupus	0.77	0.18	0.77	0.76	1.98	63.92
Paralichthys oblongus	0.74	0	0.76	0.82	1.94	65.86
Glyptocephalus cynoglossus	0.72	3.3	0.73	0.73	1.89	67.75
Alosa aestivalis	0.25	0.07	0.71	0.79	1.83	69.58
Hemitripterus americanus	6.14	0.51	0.7	0.7	1.81	71.39
Tautogolabrus adspersus	0.67	0	0.67	0.72	1.73	73.11
Myxine glutinosa	0.03	0.2	0.67	0.76	1.72	74.83
Enchelyopus cimbrius	0	0.11	0.65	0.7	1.66	76.49
Lumpenus maculatus	0	0.53	0.59	0.7	1.52	78.01
Lycenchelys verrilli	0	0.07	0.59	0.7	1.52	79.53
Argentina striata	0	0.2	0.59	0.7	1.52	81.04

Appendix 9. SIMPER results for comparison of hotspot group 2 versus hotspot group 1 at the 20 km spatial scale. Twenty-nine species contributed to 80 % dissimilarity.

Species	Av.Abund Group2	Av.Abund Group1	Av.Diss	Diss/SD	Contrib%	Cum.%
Lepophidium profundorum	0	0.31	1.16	21.69	5.13	5.13
Lumpenus lumpretaeformis	0	0.62	1.16	21.69	5.13	10.25
Lumpenus maculatus	0.11	3.07	0.93	1.94	4.11	14.37
Maurolicus weitzmani	0.12	0	0.81	1.49	3.58	17.95
Dipturus laevis	0.1	0	0.69	1.19	3.04	20.98
Tautogolabrus adspersus	0.14	0.8	0.59	0.97	2.62	23.6
Prionotus carolinus	0.26	0	0.58	0.97	2.57	26.18
Myoxocephalus aenaeus	0.13	0.03	0.58	0.97	2.56	28.74
Artediellus Sp	0.07	0.02	0.58	0.97	2.56	31.3
Pomatomus saltatrix	0.01	0.03	0.58	0.97	2.56	33.87
Stenotomus chrysops	0.08	0.01	0.58	0.97	2.56	36.43
Urophycis regia	0.01	0.01	0.58	0.97	2.56	38.99
Lycenchelys verrilli	0.01	0.07	0.58	0.97	2.56	41.56
Malacoraja senta	0.71	0.28	0.58	0.97	2.56	44.12
Melanostigma atlanticum	0	0.01	0.58	0.97	2.56	46.68
Morone saxatilis	0.16	0.01	0.58	0.97	2.56	49.25
Cryptacanthodes maculatus	0	0.11	0.58	0.97	2.56	51.81
Gasterosteus aculeatus	0.02	0.01	0.58	0.97	2.56	54.38
Ammodytes americanus	0	0.29	0.58	0.97	2.56	56.94
Ariomma bondi	0	0.01	0.58	0.97	2.56	59.5
Brosme brosme	0.11	0.02	0.58	0.97	2.56	62.07
Ulvaria subbifurcata	0.03	0.41	0.58	0.97	2.56	64.63
Centropristis striata	0.02	0.01	0.58	0.97	2.56	67.19
Helicolenus dactylopterus	0.05	0	0.57	0.97	2.54	69.73
Enchelyopus cimbrius	0.3	2.76	0.48	0.8	2.12	71.85
Cyclopterus lumpus	0.04	0	0.47	0.79	2.07	73.93
Scomberesox saurus	0.05	0	0.46	0.8	2.04	75.97
Citharichthys arctifrons	0.02	0	0.46	0.8	2.04	78.01
Hippoglossus hippoglossus	0.03	0	0.46	0.79	2.02	80.03

Appendix 10. SIMPER results for comparison of hotspot group 2 versus hotspot group 3 at the 20 km spatial scale. Thirty-five species contributed to 80 % dissimilarity.

Species	Av.Abund Group2	Av.Abund Group3	Av.Diss	Diss/Sd	Contrib%	Cum.%
Cryptacanthodes maculatus	0	0.15	1	2.07	4.19	4.19
Lumpenus lumpretaeformis	0	0.38	0.97	1.91	4.09	8.28
Myoxocephalus aenaeus	0.13	0	0.72	1.19	3.03	11.31
Dipturus laevis	0.1	0.01	0.69	1.14	2.91	14.21
Lumpenus maculatus	0.11	1.77	0.66	1.09	2.79	17.01
Cyclopterus lumpus	0.04	0.08	0.65	1.07	2.75	19.75
Ammodytes dubius	33.97	1.74	0.65	1.04	2.73	22.48
Triglops murrayi	1.95	0.12	0.64	1.04	2.71	25.2
Brosme brosme	0.11	0.11	0.62	0.99	2.59	27.79
Prionotus carolinus	0.26	0.02	0.61	0.99	2.58	30.37
Tautogolabrus adspersus	0.14	0.07	0.61	0.99	2.57	32.94
Helicolenus dactylopterus	0.05	0.02	0.61	0.99	2.56	35.5
Artediellus Sp	0.07	0.22	0.6	0.97	2.52	38.01
Ulvaria subbifurcata	0.03	0.6	0.59	0.97	2.5	40.51
Hippoglossus hippoglossus	0.03	0.09	0.59	0.96	2.49	43.01
Maurolicus weitzmani	0.12	0.16	0.58	0.93	2.42	45.43
Scomberesox saurus	0.05	0.02	0.55	0.9	2.33	47.76
Scophthalmus aquosus	1.03	0.27	0.55	0.89	2.32	50.08
Citharichthys arctifrons	0.02	0.01	0.54	0.88	2.26	52.35
Enchelyopus cimbrius	0.3	1.65	0.52	0.83	2.19	54.54
Urophycis chesteri	0.04	0	0.48	0.81	2	56.54
Stenotomus chrysops	0.08	0.03	0.47	0.79	2	58.54
Melanostigma atlanticum	0	0.06	0.44	0.76	1.87	60.41
Centropristis striata	0.02	0.01	0.44	0.75	1.87	62.28
Lycenchelys verrilli	0.01	0.06	0.43	0.74	1.82	64.1
Gasterosteus aculeatus	0.02	0.02	0.43	0.73	1.79	65.89
Syngnathus fuscus	0.03	0.01	0.42	0.72	1.79	67.67
Alosa aestivalis	1.48	1.98	0.42	0.72	1.78	69.45
Myxine glutinosa	0.21	0.2	0.41	0.69	1.71	71.16
Paralichthys oblongus	1.44	0.45	0.4	0.67	1.67	72.83
Alosa sapidissima	0.12	0.44	0.39	0.68	1.66	74.49
Aspidophoroides monopterygius	0.55	0.34	0.39	0.67	1.66	76.15
Petromyzon marinus	0.02	0	0.39	0.68	1.64	77.8
Leucoraja erinacea	4.19	1.12	0.39	0.67	1.63	79.42
Liparis atlanticus	0.02	0	0.36	0.65	1.53	80.96

Appendix 11. SIMPER results for comparison of hotspot group 3 versus hotspot group 1 at 20 km spatial scale. Twenty-nine species contributed to 80 % dissimilarity.

Species	Av.Abund Group 3	Av.Abund Group 1	Av.Diss	Diss/SD	Contrib%	Cum.%
Lepophidium profundorum	0.01	0.31	1.05	2.85	5.16	5.16
Cyclopterus lumpus	0.08	0	0.79	1.45	3.85	9.01
Tautogolabrus adspersus	0.07	0.8	0.68	1.15	3.35	12.36
Maurolicus weitzmani	0.16	0	0.67	1.15	3.3	15.66
Ammodytes dubius	1.74	987.61	0.63	1.04	3.09	18.75
Triglops murrayi	0.12	0.06	0.63	1.04	3.06	21.81
Melanostigma atlanticum	0.06	0.01	0.59	0.98	2.87	24.69
Pomatomus saltatrix	0.01	0.03	0.59	0.98	2.87	27.56
Stenotomus chrysops	0.03	0.01	0.59	0.98	2.87	30.43
Ulvaria subbifurcata	0.6	0.41	0.59	0.98	2.87	33.31
Urophycis regia	0.04	0.01	0.59	0.98	2.87	36.18
Malacoraja senta	0.41	0.28	0.59	0.98	2.87	39.05
Morone saxatilis	0	0.01	0.59	0.98	2.87	41.93
Myoxocephalus aenaeus	0	0.03	0.59	0.98	2.87	44.8
Ammodytes americanus	0	0.29	0.59	0.98	2.87	47.68
Ariomma bondi	0	0.01	0.59	0.98	2.87	50.55
Artediellus Sp	0.22	0.02	0.59	0.98	2.87	53.42
Centropristis striata	0.01	0.01	0.59	0.98	2.87	56.3
Lycenchelys verrilli	0.06	0.07	0.59	0.98	2.87	59.17
Cryptacanthodes maculatus	0.15	0.11	0.59	0.98	2.87	62.04
Gasterosteus aculeatus	0.02	0.01	0.59	0.98	2.87	64.92
Brosme brosme	0.11	0.02	0.59	0.98	2.87	67.79
Lumpenus maculatus	1.77	3.07	0.51	0.84	2.48	70.27
Hippoglossus hippoglossus	0.09	0	0.5	0.84	2.43	72.7
Scophthalmus aquosus	0.27	0.47	0.44	0.75	2.15	74.85
Paralichthys oblongus	0.45	0.83	0.38	0.67	1.86	76.71
Aspidophoroides monopterygius	0.34	1.18	0.32	0.59	1.57	78.28
Leucoraja erinacea	1.12	1.33	0.31	0.59	1.53	79.8
Scomberesox saurus	0.02	0	0.31	0.59	1.5	81.3

Appendix 12. SIMPER results for comparison of hotspot group 1 versus hotspot group 2 at the 40 km spatial scale. Thirty-five species contributed to 80 % dissimilarity.

Species	Av.Abund Group1	Av.Abund Group2	Av.Diss	Diss/SD	Contrib%	Cum.%
Lumpenus maculatus	0	3.1	0.88	16.05	4.33	4.33
Helicolenus dactylopterus	0.24	0.01	0.68	1.68	3.35	7.68
Syngnathus fuscus	0.02	0	0.67	1.67	3.28	10.96
Stenotomus chrysops	0.01	0.02	0.66	1.66	3.24	14.2
Petromyzon marinus	0.02	0	0.66	1.66	3.21	17.41
Scomberesox saurus	0.05	0	0.56	1.25	2.75	20.16
Urophycis regia	0	0.1	0.55	1.24	2.7	22.86
Dipturus laevis	0.06	0.01	0.55	1.24	2.69	25.55
Merluccius albidus	0	0.03	0.55	1.24	2.68	28.22
Maurolicus weitzmani	0.05	0.13	0.46	0.97	2.23	30.45
Prionotus carolinus	0.17	0.01	0.45	0.97	2.22	32.67
Pomatomus saltatrix	0.02	0.01	0.45	0.96	2.21	34.89
Hippoglossus hippoglossus	0.02	0.03	0.45	0.97	2.21	37.09
Argentina silus	0.9	0.01	0.45	0.97	2.21	39.3
Myoxocephalus aenaeus	0.12	0.02	0.45	0.97	2.19	41.49
Ulvaria subbifurcata	0.04	1.97	0.45	0.96	2.19	43.68
Gasterosteus aculeatus	0.02	0.03	0.45	0.96	2.19	45.87
Citharichthys arctifrons	0.02	0	0.44	0.97	2.18	48.04
Paralichthys dentatus	0.01	0.01	0.44	0.96	2.17	50.22
Torpedo nobiliana	0	0.01	0.44	0.96	2.17	52.39
Melanostigma atlanticum	0.04	0.09	0.44	0.97	2.16	54.55
Pholis gunnellus	0.01	0.01	0.44	0.97	2.16	56.71
Urophycis chesteri	0.31	0.02	0.44	0.97	2.16	58.87
Nemichthys scolopaceus	0	0	0.44	0.96	2.14	61.01
Liparis atlanticus	0.03	0	0.44	0.96	2.14	63.15
Lumpenus lumpretaeformis	0	0.67	0.44	0.96	2.14	65.29
Lepophidium profundorum	0	0.09	0.43	0.96	2.11	67.4
Brevoortia tyrannus	0	0.01	0.43	0.96	2.1	69.5
Mallotus villosus	0	0.04	0.42	0.96	2.08	71.58
Lycenchelys verrilli	0.01	0.02	0.34	0.75	1.65	73.23
Myoxocephalus scorpius	0	0.01	0.33	0.75	1.62	74.84
Centropristis striata	0.04	0.02	0.33	0.75	1.62	76.46
Morone saxatilis	0.14	0	0.32	0.75	1.58	78.03
Ariomma bondi	0	0	0.32	0.75	1.58	79.61
Ammodytes americanus	0.39	0.04	0.32	0.75	1.58	81.19

NMSP CONSERVATION SERIES PUBLICATIONS

To date, the following reports have been published in the Marine Sanctuaries Conservation Series. All publications are available on the Office of National Marine Sanctuaries website (http://www.sanctuaries.noaa.gov/).

Examples of Ecosystem-Based Management in National Marine Sanctuaries: Moving from Theory to Practice (ONMS-10-02)

The Application Of Observing System Data In California Current Ecosystem Assessments (ONMS-10-01)

Reconciling Ecosystem-Based Management and Focal Resource Conservation in the Papahānaumokuākea Marine National Monument (ONMS-09-04)

Preliminary Comparison of Natural Versus Model-predicted Recovery of Vessel-generated Seagrass Injuries in Florida Keys National Marine Sanctuary (ONMS-09-03)

A Comparison of Seafloor Habitats and Associated Benthic Fauna in Areas Open and Closed to Bottom Trawling Along the Central California Continental Shelf (ONMS-09-02)

Chemical Contaminants, Pathogen Exposure and General Health Status of Live and Beach-Cast Washington Sea Otters (*Enhydra lutris kenyoni*) (ONMS-09-01)

Caribbean Connectivity: Implications for Marine Protected Area Management (ONMS-08-07)

Knowledge, Attitudes and Perceptions of Management Strategies and Regulations of FKNMS by Commercial Fishers, Dive Operators, and Environmental Group Members: A Baseline Characterization and 10-year Comparison (ONMS-08-06)

First Biennial Ocean Climate Summit: Finding Solutions for San Francisco Bay Area's Coast and Ocean (ONMS-08-05)

A Scientific Forum on the Gulf of Mexico: The Islands in the Stream Concept (NMSP-08-04)

M/V *ELPIS* Coral Reef Restoration Monitoring Report Monitoring Events 2004-2007 Florida Keys National Marine Sanctuary Monroe County, Florida (NMSP-08-03)

CONNECTIVITY Science, People and Policy in the Florida Keys National Marine Sanctuary (NMSP-08-02)

M/V *ALEC OWEN MAITLAND* Coral Reef Restoration Monitoring Report Monitoring Events 2004-2007 Florida Keys National Marine Sanctuary Monroe County, Florida (NMSP-08-01)

Automated, objective texture segmentation of multibeam echosounder data - Seafloor survey and substrate maps from James Island to Ozette Lake, Washington Outer Coast. (NMSP-07-05)

Observations of Deep Coral and Sponge Assemblages in Olympic Coast National Marine Sanctuary, Washington (NMSP-07-04)

A Bioregional Classification of the Continental Shelf of Northeastern North America for Conservation Analysis and Planning Based on Representation (NMSP-07-03)

M/V *WELLWOOD* Coral Reef Restoration Monitoring Report Monitoring Events 2004-2006 Florida Keys National Marine Sanctuary Monroe County, Florida (NMSP-07-02)

Survey report of NOAA Ship McArthur II cruises AR-04-04, AR-05-05 and AR-06-03: Habitat classification of side scan sonar imagery in support of deep-sea coral/sponge explorations at the Olympic Coast National Marine Sanctuary (NMSP-07-01)

2002 - 03 Florida Keys National Marine Sanctuary Science Report: An Ecosystem Report Card After Five Years of Marine Zoning (NMSP-06-12)

Habitat Mapping Effort at the Olympic Coast National Marine Sanctuary - Current Status and Future Needs (NMSP-06-11)

M/V *CONNECTED* Coral Reef Restoration Monitoring Report Monitoring Events 2004-2005 Florida Keys National Marine Sanctuary Monroe County, Florida (NMSP-06-010)

M/V *JACQUELYN L* Coral Reef Restoration Monitoring Report Monitoring Events 2004-2005 Florida Keys National Marine Sanctuary Monroe County, Florida (NMSP-06-09)

M/V *WAVE WALKER* Coral Reef Restoration Baseline Monitoring Report - 2004 Florida Keys National Marine Sanctuary Monroe County, Florida (NMSP-06-08)

Olympic Coast National Marine Sanctuary Habitat Mapping: Survey report and classification of side scan sonar data from surveys HMPR-114-2004-02 and HMPR-116-2005-01 (NMSP-06-07)

A Pilot Study of Hogfish (*Lachnolaimus maximus* Walbaum 1792) Movement in the Conch Reef Research Only Area (Northern Florida Keys) (NMSP-06-06)

Comments on Hydrographic and Topographic LIDAR Acquisition and Merging with Multibeam Sounding Data Acquired in the Olympic Coast National Marine Sanctuary (ONMS-06-05)

Conservation Science in NOAA's National Marine Sanctuaries: Description and Recent Accomplishments (ONMS-06-04)

Normalization and characterization of multibeam backscatter: Koitlah Point to Point of the Arches, Olympic Coast National Marine Sanctuary - Survey HMPR-115-2004-03 (ONMS-06-03)

Developing Alternatives for Optimal Representation of Seafloor Habitats and Associated Communities in Stellwagen Bank National Marine Sanctuary (ONMS-06-02)

Benthic Habitat Mapping in the Olympic Coast National Marine Sanctuary (ONMS-06-01)

Channel Islands Deep Water Monitoring Plan Development Workshop Report (ONMS-05-05)

Movement of yellowtail snapper (*Ocyurus chrysurus* Block 1790) and black grouper (*Mycteroperca bonaci* Poey 1860) in the northern Florida Keys National Marine Sanctuary as determined by acoustic telemetry (MSD-05-4)

The Impacts of Coastal Protection Structures in California's Monterey Bay National Marine Sanctuary (MSD-05-3)

An annotated bibliography of diet studies of fish of the southeast United States and Gray's Reef National Marine Sanctuary (MSD-05-2)

Noise Levels and Sources in the Stellwagen Bank National Marine Sanctuary and the St. Lawrence River Estuary (MSD-05-1)

Biogeographic Analysis of the Tortugas Ecological Reserve (MSD-04-1)

A Review of the Ecological Effectiveness of Subtidal Marine Reserves in Central California (MSD-04-2, MSD-04-3)

Pre-Construction Coral Survey of the M/V Wellwood Grounding Site (MSD-03-1)

Olympic Coast National Marine Sanctuary: Proceedings of the 1998 Research Workshop, Seattle, Washington (MSD-01-04)

Workshop on Marine Mammal Research & Monitoring in the National Marine Sanctuaries (MSD-01-03)

A Review of Marine Zones in the Monterey Bay National Marine Sanctuary (MSD-01-2)

Distribution and Sighting Frequency of Reef Fishes in the Florida Keys National Marine Sanctuary (MSD-01-1)

Flower Garden Banks National Marine Sanctuary: A Rapid Assessment of Coral, Fish, and Algae Using the AGRRA Protocol (MSD-00-3)

The Economic Contribution of Whalewatching to Regional Economies: Perspectives From Two National Marine Sanctuaries (MSD-00-2)

Olympic Coast National Marine Sanctuary Area to be Avoided Education and Monitoring Program (MSD-00-1)

Multi-species and Multi-interest Management: an Ecosystem Approach to Market Squid (*Loligo opalescens*) Harvest in California (MSD-99-1)